the big book of

PORN

the big book of

PORΠ

★ A PENETRATING LOOK AT ★
THE WORLD OF DIRTY MOVIES

by Seth Grahame-Smith

QUIRK BOOKS

PHILADELPHIA

Library of Congress Cataloging in Publication
  Number: 2005922080

ISBN: 1-59474-040-2

Printed in Singapore

Typeset in Helvetica Neue Extended

Designed by Bryn Ashburn

Illustrations by Jon Rogers

photography credits appear on page 207.

Distributed in North America by Chronicle Books
85 Second Street
San Francisco, CA 94105

10 9 8 7 6 5 4 3 2 1

Quirk Books
215 Church Street
Philadelphia, PA 19106
www.quirkbooks.com

dedication

To that first sun-faded
dirty magazine I found
in the woods as a boy.
I owe you so much . . .

☆contents

I remember the apocalypse.

Like hundreds of millions around the world, I was glued to the television on February 1, 2004—a calm winter's day. A fine day for football. Surrounded by friends (mostly New England transplants, like me), my spirits were soaring. And why not? Our beloved Pats were up 14–10 at the half. Confident, we turned our attention to eating onion dip and slinging insults at the always-atrocious halftime show. All was right with the world.

And then we saw it.

Janet Jackson's bejeweled breast, hanging there like an omen—a harbinger of Satan's fury.

A flash of light and a *whoosh* of hot air filled the room. I turned and saw only smoke and ash where two dear friends had sat moments before. Like so many on that fateful day, they'd spontaneously combusted—vaporized by the shock of seeing nudity on live television.

Minutes later (as we vacuumed the sofa) news reports started flooding in from around the globe: In Europe, fire-breathing antelope were swooping from the sky and snatching babies right out of their cribs. In New York, the Statue of Liberty walked into Manhattan and performed acts of unspeakable lewdness with the Chrysler Building. In Australia, Kylie Minogue began work on a new album.

It was, simply, hell on earth.

At least it *seemed* that way in the weeks and months that followed. Okay—to my knowledge, there were no deaths as a direct result of that infamous "wardrobe malfunction," but there were some very real consequences. CBS was fined a record $550,000 for allowing a nipple to befoul America's living rooms. NBC chose to cut the image of an elderly woman's breast from its hit show *ER*. ABC nervously added a delay to the Academy Awards. And to top it all off, a Tennessee woman filed suit against Jackson, CBS, and its parent company, Viacom, alleging that the halftime incident had caused her to "suffer outrage, anger, embarrassment, and serious injury." *Serious injury?*

Prudishness, it seemed, was back in fashion. And personally speaking, the timing couldn't have been worse. That's because I'd just agreed to write a book about something very near and dear to my heart—*pornos*. I was screwed. Ruined. I'd be dragged through the streets. Burned at the stake. Anti-porn activists were already seizing on "Nipplegate" to push for tougher censorship laws. What would they do when they got their hands on me?

I had no choice. Somehow, I'd have to show the masses that smut wasn't the enemy. That porn, if you'll excuse me, fills a hole in our lives. I'd combat their fears by sharing everything there was to know about dirty movies—their history, their classics, their icons . . . hell, I'd even teach them how to *make* one. Determined, I clung to a scrap of hope from an episode of *60 Minutes*: More Americans watched porno movies than sporting events. I had to have *some* allies out there.

It's taken eleven months and the bulk of my family fortune, but here it is— a tool for turning frightened pornophobes into proud pornophiles. I only pray I'm not too late.

After all, if I can save just one person from vaporizing the next time they see a naked breast, then it's all been worth it.

a brief history of porn movies

If there's pornography in your house, it's probably not sitting on a shelf in the living room for the in-laws to see. Of course it isn't. It's hidden in your sock drawer, or in the back of your closet, or in a password-protected file on your computer. A file named "receipts" because you're so clever. And that tape or DVD? The one you've watched so many times that you've memorized the minutes and seconds of your favorite parts on the display counter? I'll bet you didn't walk into a store and buy it. Nope—you borrowed (i.e., stole) it from a friend or roommate because going into a store and buying porn is so . . . weird.

Such is the double life of the porn enthusiast: outwardly embarrassed, inwardly excited. But don't feel bad. This moral wrestling match was going on long before your time. Step into the porn portal, and I'll show you what I mean . . .

We humans have always been obsessed with doing the nasty. And we've always used the arts to depict that obsession, whether through oil paintings, literature, or theater. Hell, as early as 25,000 B.C. we were decorating our caves with engravings of vaginas.

But let's face it: There's only so much masturbatory mileage you can get out of a cavewoman's hoo-ha. It would take the invention of a whole new medium—the motion picture—to usher in porn's golden age. Here are some key moments that I found stuffed between the mattresses of history.

1839

Robert Cornelius is both photographer and subject of the first-known daguerreotype taken in the United States, seen here. Who knew people had such cool hair in 1839?

1727

German professor Johann Heinrich Schulze discovers that silver nitrate darkens when it's exposed to sunlight—a breakthrough that will eventually lead to motion pictures (silver nitrate remains the key ingredient in all photographic film to this day).

1827

French aristocrat Joseph Nicéphore Niepce produces the world's first permanent photographic image. Exposure time? A mere eight hours. However, following his death in 1833, Niepce's partner—Louis Daguerre—promptly takes all the credit and renames the process the "daguerreotype." You got punked, Niepce!

1850

There are some seventy daguerreotype studios in New York City, mainly devoted to taking portraits for the aristocrats who can afford them. Not yet available: pull-down backdrops with cool blue laser beams.

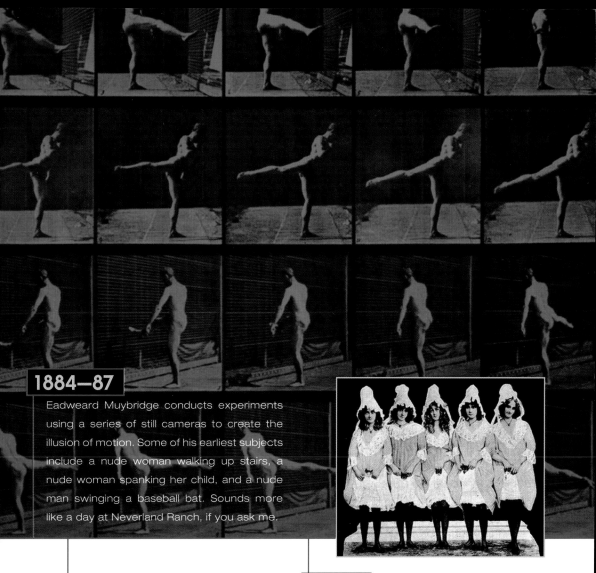

1884–87

Eadweard Muybridge conducts experiments using a series of still cameras to create the illusion of motion. Some of his earliest subjects include a nude woman walking up stairs, a nude woman spanking her child, and a nude man swinging a baseball bat. Sounds more like a day at Neverland Ranch, if you ask me.

1889

Thomas Edison perfects the kineto-scope, a device capable of recording motion pictures. Meanwhile, George Eastman (founder of Eastman Kodak) and Hannibal W. Goodwin (an American clergyman) compete to perfect flexible films that can be used in motion-picture cameras. Can you guess who wins? (Hint: Go to the nearest drugstore and ask for a roll of Hannibal film. Observe dumbfounded look on salesperson's face.)

1890s

Danish vaudevillians the Barrison Sisters (shown above) push the limits of decency on stage. The girls coyly ask the audience, *"Would you like to see our pussies?"* then lift their skirts—revealing live kittens strapped over their naughty bits. England's Machinson Sisters later steal the kitten-crotch routine, but add a song, with lyrics that include: *"Would you give me the tip of it . . . because I've got a pussycat . . . who hasn't eaten that?"* (For the record, the ASPCA was founded in 1866—where are those guys when you need them?)

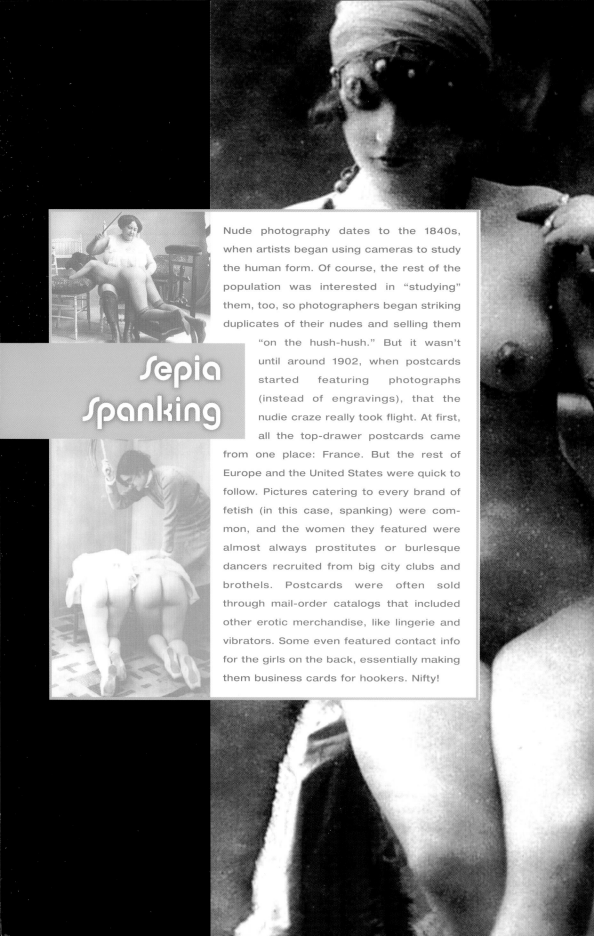

Sepia Spanking

Nude photography dates to the 1840s, when artists began using cameras to study the human form. Of course, the rest of the population was interested in "studying" them, too, so photographers began striking duplicates of their nudes and selling them "on the hush-hush." But it wasn't until around 1902, when postcards started featuring photographs (instead of engravings), that the nudie craze really took flight. At first, all the top-drawer postcards came from one place: France. But the rest of Europe and the United States were quick to follow. Pictures catering to every brand of fetish (in this case, spanking) were common, and the women they featured were almost always prostitutes or burlesque dancers recruited from big city clubs and brothels. Postcards were often sold through mail-order catalogs that included other erotic merchandise, like lingerie and vibrators. Some even featured contact info for the girls on the back, essentially making them business cards for hookers. Nifty!

1894

Edison begins producing short films. Over the next few years, some of his more provocative titles will include *What Happened in the Tunnel*, *Seminary Girls*, and *Aunt Sallie's Wonderful Bustle*. *Tunnel* features a man groping a female passenger on a train. *Seminary* is little more than a pillow fight between schoolgirls in their nightgowns. In *Bustle*, Aunt Sallie's hat is blown off while she stands on a bridge. She leans over to retrieve it and falls—but luckily she lands on her bulbous ass, which is so rotund that it gently bounces her back onto the bridge, hat and all.

1897

Georges Méliès makes *Après le Bal—le Tub (After the Ball—the Tub)*, in which a voluptuous young nude is lovingly bathed by her maid. Five years later, Méliès films his masterpiece *A Trip to the Moon*, a sci-fi adventure with then-groundbreaking special effects. In one scene, scantily clad chorus girls push a long, hard rocket into the launch chamber. Scandalous!

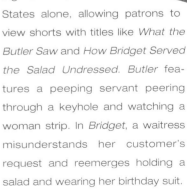

1905

The first nickelodeons (coin-operated machines for viewing short films) appear. Within two years, there are five thousand operating in the United States alone, allowing patrons to view shorts with titles like *What the Butler Saw* and *How Bridget Served the Salad Undressed*. *Butler* features a peeping servant peering through a keyhole and watching a woman strip. In *Bridget*, a waitress misunderstands her customer's request and reemerges holding a salad and wearing her birthday suit.

1896

In the creatively titled *The Kiss*, May Irwin and John C. Rice share the first filmed smooch—a gentle peck on the lips pictured here. In fact, *Kiss* is nothing more than a reenactment of a scene from *The Widow Jones*, a stage play (also starring Irwin and Rice). A mere twenty seconds long, it's one of the first movies ever screened for the public, and gets savaged by one critic as "absolutely disgusting." In Ottawa, Canada, calls for police interference go unanswered. (That's no joke, dear reader—there are actual calls for police interference.)

1915

The U.S. Supreme Court denies First Amendment protection to films, deciding that they're "a business pure and simple, originated and conducted for profit" and "capable of evil." The decision convinces many in Hollywood that a standard of self-censorship is necessary to keep Washington at bay.

1907

El Sartorio, the earliest surviving porno, is produced in Argentina. Up to this point, there's been plenty of nudity and erotica in film, but there's been a conspicuous absence of actual sex. *Sartorio* changes that. It tells the story of three young women bathing, splashing, and cavorting about in a river. Naturally, their cavorting leads to some girl-on-girl action. But wait! Suddenly, the devil himself (some guy in a cheap costume) appears, captures one of the women, and forces her to go down on him. Then it's on to the sex, which is graphically portrayed through the world's first "piston shots" (see page 178).

1915   limp moment in porn history

While the racist epic *The Birth of a Nation* is thrilling audiences and rubbing salt in Civil War wounds, another new release is preaching love and kindness to strangers. Okay, so you couldn't see this film in any "reputable" movie house. You'd have to visit a makeshift theater like the one pictured above. Still, *A Free Ride* is widely considered the best example of the early American "stag"—that is, a short film meant for adult male eyes only. In *Ride,* our male hero picks up two female hitchhikers and takes them for a scenic daytime drive. When he stops to pee, the girls spy on him and become aroused. He returns the favor, spying on his passengers while *they* pee. It isn't long before this voyeurism turns into a full-fledged three-way of graphically depicted sex. Behold the erotic power of urination!

Mutascopes featured rotating flip cards that simulated movement. Racy plots and glimpses of flesh made them very popular in the early twentieth century.

Today, hard-core porn is always a mouse click away. But back in 1915, skin flicks weren't just hard to come by—they were downright illegal. To get their fix, our granddaddies had to wait for a stag master to pull into town. These one-man circuses drove all over the country, their cars packed with film canisters and a projector.

Stag Films Carry the Torch

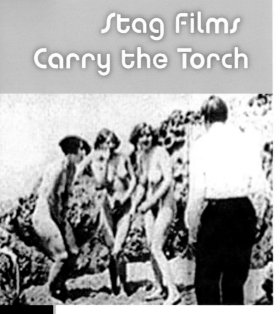

They'd pop into the local bar or fraternity house and quietly advertise their wares. Usually the same night, all the horny men within a nuclear mile would pay admission and pack themselves into a makeshift theater—whether it was an Elks lodge, a private home, or an actual movie palace after hours.

Then, the air thick with cigar smoke and repressed sexuality, they'd whoop and holler through a series of stag films—silent, black-and-white shorts that rarely bothered with plots or production values. It was even common for the "actors" to wear masks to protect their identities. One stag, *Country Stud Horse* (1920), ends with a crew member throwing a towel on top of the on-camera couple. The film continues to roll while the woman cleans herself up and the man sits around looking bored. Ah, cinema!

Still, while they may have been awful, stags were also incredibly important. From the birth of movies to the 1960s, they were the only way most Americans could get their porno fix. With some help from William Rotsler's *Contemporary Erotic Cinema*, I've categorized the stories of most stag films into five basic categories:

Plot 1: A woman is home alone. She happens upon something phallic and gets turned on by playing with it. A man conveniently shows up, and some "doing it" ensues.

Plot 2: A farm girl gets turned on watching animals have sex. She grabs the nearest farmhand and hops on his pitchfork.

Plot 3: A doctor examines a young woman. Diagnosis? She's in need of an immediate injection. "Injection!" Get it? A hot beef inject . . . oh, never mind.

Plot 4: A burglar gets more than he bargained for when he finds a young woman asleep in her bed.

Plot 5: A man discovers a female sunbather or skinny-dipper (as in *Getting His Goat*, shown above). Again, some "doing it" ensues.

As proof that porn is environmentally conscious, most of these plots continue to be recycled today.

☆ whoray for hollywood!

As Hollywood got bigger, so did its shadow. Porn was moving into adolescence—an awkward phase that would bring its share of challenges and conflicts, and ultimately a sexual awakening that marked the beginning of its adulthood.

1916

Screen beauty Annette Kellerman, famous for her daringly skimpy bathing suits, decides to forego the suits altogether in *A Daughter of the Gods* (a still from this film forms the background of this page). Thirty-six years later, Kellerman's life story is told in the film *Million Dollar Mermaid*, starring another swimming beauty—Esther Williams. Much to the chagrin of male movie-goers, Williams opts to keep her suit firmly fastened.

1921

Allen Holubar's epic *Man, Woman, Marriage* features the Emperor Constantine in his harem, surrounded by a bevy of lusty, naked beauties. The film exploits a clever loophole in the decency standards of the time: Nudity on its own? Wrong. Nudity depicting the depravity of pre-Christian savages? Righteous.

1922 — limp moment in porn history

The sensational trials of "Fatty" Arbuckle (shown here) and other entertainers portray Hollywood as a mecca of immorality, both on screen and off. To combat this negative image, the Motion Picture Producers and Distributors Association is formed. The group allows Hollywood to police both its movies *and* its stars' behavior. The association is headed by former Postmaster General William Hays—a name that will become synonymous with censorship.

1932 — limp moment in porn history

Joe Breen, a staunch Irish Catholic who is later appointed to head the Production Code Administration, writes a private letter/rant on Hollywood's sinful climate: "Sexual perversion is rampant. Any number of our directors and stars are perverts. These Jews seem to think of nothing but moneymaking and sexual indulgence. . . . The men and women who engage in this sort of business are the men and women who decide what the film fare of the nation is to be. . . . Ninety-five percent of these folks are Jews of an Eastern European lineage. They are, probably, the scum of the earth."

19

1933 — limp moment in porn history

Jerry Falwell is born on August 11. The good reverend has spent years blaming pornography as one of the ills responsible for the decline of Western civilization—failing to realize that pornography was thriving long before Western civilization sprouted legs and crawled out of the ocean. Now, I'm sure the reverend is a decent man, and I know he stands by his convictions (like when he supported segregation in the 1950s). But it's hard to get behind his anti-porn rallying cry when he also believes that homosexuality brought about the September 11 terrorist attacks. (Under tremendous pressure, he later apologized for the assertion.)

1939—45

Funny how a madman and his legions of doom can make people care less about nipples. As World War II raged across their continent, Europeans found themselves a little preoccupied—you know, with staying alive—and thus a little less concerned with on-screen kisses or the utterance of filthy words like "damn." This loosening of restrictions begins to seep into the United States, which at the time had the world's harshest decency standards for films.

1933

Prior to becoming a mainstream starlet, Hedy Lamarr goes topless in the European art film *Extase*. The movie is rife with orgasmic metaphors and suggestive close-ups, a fact that leads Hedy's then-husband, Fritz Mandl, to buy and destroy every print he can get his hands on. He fails. The film goes on to international acclaim, and Hedy goes on to Hollywood stardom.

1934 — limp moment in porn history

Some filmmakers refuse to abide by the Hays Code. In response, the National Legion of Catholic Decency organizes boycotts of films that don't measure up. The boycott is so effective that Hollywood quickly buckles, agreeing to a new policy of strict enforcement. To receive national distribution, all films must now receive a seal of approval from the Production Code Administration.

The Hays Code of 1930

When the Hays Code—a set of regulations dictating what American films can and cannot show—is formally adopted by the Motion Picture Producers and Distributors Association, it's first perceived as an empty threat—a way to temper Hollywood's immoral image and keep politicians happy. But a boycott will change all that four years later (see page 20). Some memorable guidelines from the Hays Code include the following:

★ "Excessive and lustful kissing, lustful embraces, suggestive postures and gestures, are not to be shown." The accepted standard for "excessive" was anything longer than four feet of film (about two and a half seconds). By comparison, today's porn standards classify "excessive" as any part of the anatomy longer than four feet.

★ "Complete nudity is never permitted. This includes nudity in fact or in silhouette, or any lecherous or licentious notice thereof by other characters in the picture." Bad: Seeing boobies. Worse: Seeing someone see someone else's boobies.

★ "No picture shall be produced which will lower the moral standards of those who see it."

★ "The effect of nudity or semi-nudity upon the normal man or woman . . . has been honestly recognized by all lawmakers and moralists."

★ "Sex hygiene and venereal diseases are not subjects for motion pictures."

★ "White slavery shall not be treated." Slavery of all other races, however, was apparently A-OK.

1943

The posters for Howard Hughes's *The Outlaw* feature star Jane Russell in various seductive poses and make no attempt to downplay her gigantic, um, costars. As a result, the film's seal of approval is revoked. Hughes says to hell with it and distributes the film himself—using the controversy to market it as "Howard Hughes' Daring Production." The campaign works—audiences flock to see *Outlaw*, spurred in part by a judge's proclamation that Russell's breasts "hung over the picture like a thunderstorm spread over a landscape."

1946

Japanese prostitutes—in an attempt to appear "more American" to the occupying GIs—start having silicone injected directly into their breasts. Despite the possibility of sickness (not to mention death), the practice becomes hugely popular, even spreading to the United States. It's a crude forerunner of the modern silicone implants that will become popular in the late 1970s.

1943

Director and choreographer Busby Berkeley flies in the face of the Hays Code with a dance number in *The Gang's All Here*. He equips each of his trademark chorus girls with a gigantic banana, which he has them thrust from their scantily clad pelvises in something resembling a bizarre penis-worship ritual.

1953

The first issue of Hugh Hefner's *Playboy* hits American newsstands. Featuring a topless Marilyn Monroe as its first centerfold, the men's mag sells an impressive 54,175 copies at 50 cents apiece. Of course, a lot's changed since then. Today, *Playboy* sells more than three million copies a month in the United States—at a cover price of $5.99.

1957

Roth v. United States goes before the U.S. Supreme Court. Samuel Roth is a New York–based smut peddler convicted for mailing obscene advertisements and books. The court rules that obscenity is not protected under the First Amendment, and Roth loses his appeal. But in issuing the court's decision, Justice William Brennan writes: "Sex and obscenity are not synonymous . . . The portrayal of sex, e.g., in art, literature and scientific works, is not itself sufficient reason to deny material the constitutional protection of freedom of speech and press." Brennan also writes that for materials to be denied First Amendment protection, they have to be "utterly without redeeming social importance." That last sentence may not sound like much, but in fact, it changes everything. Suddenly, if you can argue that a movie (or picture, or book) has even a *little* "social importance," it's guaranteed protection under the First Amendment.

1964

Reuben Sturman is America's "godfather of porn." A former Ohio magazine salesman who realizes that nudie mags are selling like hotcakes, Sturman uses his entrepreneurial skill to build the country's biggest smut empire. FBI agents raid Sturman's warehouse and indict him on federal obscenity charges. Never one to shy away from a courtroom, Sturman turns around and sues FBI Director J. Edgar Hoover for violating his civil rights. The charges against Sturman are dropped, though the government will eventually convict him of tax evasion twenty-eight years later.

1959

Russ Meyer is a World War II newsreel cameraman who finds work as one of *Playboy* magazine's first photographers—a job well suited to his taste for busty women. But shooting centerfolds soon evolves into shooting films, and 1959's *The Immoral Mr. Teas*—his first important work—is a box-office hit. Meyer's ability to weave sex, violence, and humor is unparalleled, and his films are perfect fits for the drive-ins that dot the American landscape. He'll go on to push the envelope of decency of "mainstream" cinema through the '60s and '70s with titles

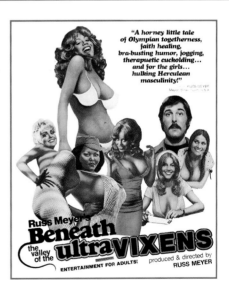

like *Mondo Topless* (1966), *Beyond the Valley of the Dolls* (cowritten by film critic Roger Ebert, 1970) and *Beneath the Valley of the Ultra-Vixens* (1979).

NOW PLAYING "THE CHEERLEADER." "X"

1968

The Hays Code is replaced by an early version of the ratings system that is still used to this day (see opposite page). Suddenly free of the old restraints, theaters in San Francisco and Los Angeles start screening "beaver films." No, not documentaries about dam-building rodents. These films feature nothing but close-ups of the female anatomy, and they are totally devoid of actual sex. Unbelievably stupid? Of course. But unbelievably important, too. For the first time in America, adults can walk into a public theater and see smut without fear of arrest. Or, personally speaking, fear of arousal.

1964–67

Lasse Braun is the "king" of European porn, famous for selling "loops" (single-reel pornos) all over the continent. Based in Copenhagen, he loads his car with smut and drives from country to country unobstructed and unsearched, thanks to his father's diplomatic license plates. But there's something else that sets Braun apart from the other traveling hucksters of his day—he also advises filmmakers on how to improve the quality of their product. Braun eventually cuts out the middleman and begins directing his own pornos, some of which (*French Blue*, *Sensations*) rank among the best of their time. He remains (along with son Axel) a force in Europe and America's adult industries to this day.

1969

Denmark legalizes all pornography. The following year, a government report shows a decrease in the number of reported sex crimes.

In 1968, the Motion Picture Association of America (MPAA) unveiled a new system of rating movies. There was G (general audiences), M (mature audiences), R (restricted audiences), and X (no one under seventeen admitted). However, the public decided that "Mature" sounded more ominous than "Restricted," so M was soon replaced by GP (General audiences, parental guidance suggested). By 1970, GP became the PG that we know and love today.

The Hijacking of "X"

At first, the system seemed to work. The X-rated *Midnight Cowboy* took home an Oscar for Best Picture in 1969. In 1971, the X-rated *A Clockwork Orange* raked in huge profits and critical acclaim. But then came the pornographers. When dirty movies went mainstream in the early '70s, the peddlers chose to release them with X ratings—even though they weren't required to do so.

According to the rules, a film that hadn't been reviewed by the MPAA could brand itself anything *but* G, M, or R—the three ratings they'd actually bothered to trademark. Unfortunately, there was nothing in the rules that said they *couldn't* use X, either. It didn't take long for X to become synonymous with porn—a fact that led some Hollywood filmmakers to release their films with *no* rating rather than accept the now-dreaded cross.

But porn had its own problems with X. It was, after all, a rating created with the mainstream in mind. "XXX" was the evolution they'd been waiting for. Never mind the fact that it was nothing more than a marketing gimmick, or that "XX" had been rudely overlooked as the natural successor. XXX remains the gold standard for all pornos to this day.

The MPAA fought back in 1990, announcing that it was dumping X in favor of NC-17. But so far (due in part to the newspapers and TV stations that won't advertise them) no NC-17 title has managed to make much of a splash at the box office.

☆ the golden decade

America had been though a decade of unprecedented social and political change in the 1960s, and the entertainment industry was struggling to stay hip. The '70s would see Ozzie and Harriet replaced by Archie and Edith; *The Waltons* evicted in favor of *The Jeffersons*. With television sets now in virtually every American household, Hollywood was hemorrhaging ticket buyers. Eventually, it succeeded in winning back its audience by offering something TV couldn't—more sex. It was the perfect time for porn to test its boundaries. And by the time the decade was over, what had long been a back-alley business would be transformed into a massive global industry.

1971

The "godfather" and the "king" meet at last. American porn tycoon Ruben Sturman travels overseas to visit his European counterpart, Lasse Braun. Sturman wants Braun's help with his new invention—the peep show booth. Throwbacks to the nickelodeon, the booths are coin-operated viewing machines with one important distinction—a locking door. Let's hear it for masturbation! With Braun providing the films and Sturman putting booths in virtually every adult bookstore in America, a billion-dollar industry is born overnight. (Exact figures aren't available, since profits from the booths are rarely reported to the government.) One thing is certain: Sturman and Braun become offensively wealthy.

1972

A pair of dirty movies changes everything. *Deep Throat* and *Behind the Green Door* (see next chapter) play to sold-out crowds across the country, bringing porn to the surface of American culture. Suddenly it's chic to be seen at an adult theater. You'll find all sorts of people standing in line—from New York's literati to suburban housewives. The mainstream media seize on the phenomenon, and the films' respective starlets, Linda Lovelace and Marilyn Chambers, become household names. Men and women buy T-shirts emblazoned with "Linda Lovelace Blows My Mind." Controversy swirls around the all-American "girl next door" Chambers, who, prior to starring in *Green Door*, was the wholesome face of the detergent Ivory Snow.

1976

JVC launches VHS, beginning a format war that divides the electronics industry into two camps—one supporting JVC, the other supporting Sony's Betamax. While Sony boasts smaller cassettes and superior picture quality, VHS has twice the recording time (two hours), not to mention the distinct advantage of being cheaper to produce. Faced with the possibility of stopping to change tapes in the middle of *Saturday Night Fever*, the public casts its vote for VHS.

1972

Last Tango in Paris is the first mainstream film to include depictions of anal sex. Now, kids—before you rush out and rent it, be warned that half of that sexual equation is a post–good looks Marlon Brando. If you watch the movie in fast-forward, I swear you can see him gaining weight.

1973

Once again the issue of what is and what isn't "obscene" reaches the Supreme court, when adult bookseller Marvin Miller is busted for mailing dirty pamphlets. In ruling on *Miller v. California*, the Court passes the hot potato by handing states the right to decide their own obscenity laws. That same year, *The Devil in Miss Jones* (see next chapter) becomes a runaway smash in adult theaters from coast to coast. So much for the states cracking down on obscenity.

☆ the party's over

The '70s were good to porn. The industry had enjoyed widespread popularity, big budgets, and relatively few life-threatening diseases. Drugs were plentiful, tight slacks fashionable, and one-night stands acceptable. But a conservative wind was blowing in America, a wind that swept Ronald Reagan into office— a new president who projected an old-school Hollywood image. Porn would continue to grow, even thrive, over the next two decades, but it would also have to deal with a three-pronged assault: increasingly conservative politics, the advent of AIDS, and new technologies that opened the business up to a new breed of amateur pornographers.

1980
limp moment in porn history

Linda Lovelace, who became a star eight years earlier with *Deep Throat*, publishes her autobiography, *Ordeal*. To say that she's had a change of heart is putting it mildly. She rails against the film's producers and director— accusing them of forcing her into making *Throat* at gunpoint (her accounts have since been widely refuted by those who knew her, and no charges were ever brought). As Linda Boreman, she becomes an anti-porn crusader and lecturer.

1986

Adult film sensation Traci Lords (at right) is making big money, driving a Mercedes, and signing autographs all over the world. Not bad for a girl who's only been making films since 1984. Just one tiny problem— she was *sixteen* in 1984. Enter the Feds, who bust Traci and use her as an excuse to investigate a long list of stars, producers, and distributors. Millions of dollars of merchandise is immediately ripped from the shelves and destroyed. Of the seventy-plus porn movies Lords made, only one can still be legally purchased in the United States. It's called *Traci, I Love You*, and it's horrible.

1982

Both JVC and Sony launch the world's first one-piece consumer camcorders. Until now, video cameras have been expensive, bulky two-piece units. With the advent of the affordable camcorder, just about anyone who wants to can make their own pornography. (Sure, affordable Super-8 cameras had been around forever, but camcorders eliminate the embarrassing step of having your film developed.)

1987

With home video cementing its hold on the adult industry, there are less than two hundred porn theaters left in the United States. That's a decline of nearly 80 percent in a single decade.

1989

Over 50 percent of American households have VCRs. Compare that to 1 percent a decade earlier. Compare, I say! The feature films of the '70s have given way to ultracheap camcorder quickies completely devoid of production values or plot. The new top-sellers are four-hour compilations, wall-to-wall sex movies, and extreme gang bangs.

1989

Male stripper John Stagliano (the guy on the left in this photo) buys a camcorder and begins shooting first-person porn movies—he later assumes the name "Buttman" and starts Evil Angel Productions. It's an early foray into what will become the biggest genre in porn: gonzo—taken from the name ascribed to Hunter S. Thompson's subjective style of journalism (see page 133). Stagliano stopped performing after testing HIV-positive in 1997, but he remains one of the busiest directors in porn.

1995

Annabel Chong does 251 men in one day, shattering porn records and making her the odds-on favorite for another world record: fastest childbirth ever. The film is so well received that it creates a sort of slutty one-upmanship. In 1996, Jasmin St. Claire takes the crown by conquering three hundred in one day. Then, in 1999, Houston (the porn star, not the city) does 620. Shhh . . . You hear that? That's the sound of 620 marriages ending.

2001

Exit Bubba. For eight years, the Clinton administration focused on everything *but* porn, and the industry was allowed to flourish. All that changes when George W. Bush selects John Ashcroft as his Attorney General. Maybe it's the fact that he opens every workday with a voluntary prayer meeting for staffers. Or maybe it was how he allegedly ordered a statue called *Spirit of Justice* (which has been around since 1936) covered with fabric because it featured an exposed breast. It's pretty obvious that this guy is no friend to porn.

1997

DVDs go consumer. The new format is a gold mine for mainstream and porn distributors alike, who can now rerelease new versions of old titles and add extra features—deleted scenes, "making of" documentaries, and a dazzling array of subtitle languages—to make new films more enticing. But there's an added bonus for pornos—the multiple-angle feature, which lets viewers flip between different cameras at will. "Wait a second, you mean I get to watch a hot girl have sex *and* direct my own movie at the same time? It's like two fantasies for the price of one!"

2004

VCA releases a musical version of its classic *The Opening of Misty Beethoven*. The updated version features a production number in which Randy Spears's dick sings "The Penis Tango."

The Forefront of Technology

Pornography has always been the tip of the technology spear, as it were. Here's how it usually goes: **(1)** "Something new" comes along. **(2)** It's used to deliver pornography, proving there's a market for this "something new." **(3)** The rest of the world gets excited and jumps on the "something new" bandwagon. Some examples:

The Printing Press: By the early 1500s, print shops have sprung up in more than 250 European cities—even though the continent remains largely illiterate. Thankfully, reading skills aren't required to appreciate Pietro Aretino's *Postures* (1524), a collection of sixteen graphic engravings depicting different sexual positions.

Photography: Some twenty years after the first daguerreotype is taken in the United States, lonely Civil War soldiers anxiously open their mail and find dirty photos from their buddies back home.

Paperback Novels: Beginning in the mid-1800s, "dime novels" bring literature to the huddled masses. The paperback's popularity is spurred by its "unrefined" fare—westerns, murder mysteries, and (you guessed it) pornography.

Motion Pictures: Not only are motion pictures *immediately* used to produce erotica (less than a year after the first movie was projected in France, actress Louise Willy went topless in a short called *The Bath*), but the stag-film industry helps drive the proliferation of the Super-8 and 16mm film formats.

VHS: The format is launched in 1976 and becomes a success, even though Blockbuster doesn't open its first location until 1985. Till then, it's doubtful that mom-and-pop video stores would have survived without their enormous pornographic profits.

Talk Radio: As a format, talk radio is virtually nonexistent before Howard Stern sets fire to the airwaves with his patent brand of sexual innuendo and raunchy humor.

The Internet: Forget the tired Al Gore jokes. Porn is responsible for the Internet as we know it. While AOL and eBay were still finding their sea legs, porn sites were making mega-profits. More importantly, they motivated more people to jump on the "information superhighway." If you're not convinced that porn is the most viable force on the Internet, consider this: I recently Googled *porn* and got 127,000,000 results. That's more than *love* (112,000,000), *money* (119,000,000), or *God* (60,200,000). Which one's most important to *you*?

CD-ROMs: Adult companies invest heavily in the new format in the mid-1990s, drawn to its interactive potential. In fact, by 1996—a year when 56 kbps modems are considered blazingly fast—the industry's biggest awards show already has multiple categories devoted to CD-ROMs.

Virtual Reality: Advances in surgery? Previsualization for architects? Training for law enforcement? Bullshit. There's only one reason the boys at MIT and Caltech are working around the clock to improve the quality of VR devices—sex. A suit that accurately mimics sex between a real person and a machine (or two real people in different places) has been called "the Holy Grail" of porn. So far, no luck. C'mon, scientists! I'm not getting any younger!

One of the most common criticisms of porn is that it doesn't contribute anything to society. Hogwash! For one, it saves really hot girls with really low self-esteem from a life of working demeaning retail jobs. Not enough? Then consider this—without porn, many of your favorite things in life would have never come to pass.

The Matrix

Skintight rubber suits, black leather, underground nightclubs, and chicks who kick ass? The Wachowski brothers (whose first directorial effort, *Bound,* was a crime thriller about a pair of hot lesbians) couldn't have made the world's most expensive S&M movie without the porn versions that came before it. By the way, following the conclusion of the *Matrix* trilogy, Larry Wachowski decided he'd rather be "Linda Wachowski"—pending an upcoming sex change operation. As Keanu would say, "Whoa."

Sex and the City

You're telling me Carrie and friends could've tackled topics like the taste of semen, vibrator addiction, penis size, and golden showers without porn paving the way? Like its smutty ancestors, *City* embraced the idea that a woman could be independent, aggressive, and best of all, love sex.

Fashion

Knee-highs, "fuck-me" pumps, mini-miniskirts, and jeans cut four inches below the top of ass cracks. All appearing at suburban shopping malls near you. And while you're out shopping, pick up some merchandise from Porn Star Clothing—a whole line dedicated to celebrating the art form. You've gotta love it. Shirts emblazoned with "Ron Jeremy for President," "Viagra is for pussies," and "Do you wanna fuck me?" The answer is yes! Yes, I do!

Teenage Sex Comedies

Jason Biggs bopping an apple pie? Cameron Diaz using semen as styling gel? Let's face it: Without porn blazing the way, teen-oriented sex comedies like

American Pie and There's Something About Mary would have never made it to the silver screen. Not to mention The Last American Virgin, My Tutor, Private Lessons, Risky Business, and the mother of all teen sex comedies, Porky's.

Madonna

It ain't the songwriting, folks (although I'm guilty of busting a little "La Isla Bonita" in the car now and then). It's the imagery—the videos, the outfits, the gyrations, and (of course) the pointy bra from the Blond Ambition tour. Before I even knew that peep shows existed, there was Madonna dancing in a faux peep show on MTV. And whether it's "Like a Virgin," "Erotica," or "Justify My Love," Our Lady of Pop is built on a foundation of sex first, music second.

"Porn-Lite" Mags

Kids have it so easy these days. When I was a wee lad, it took a Mission: Impossible–style operation to get my filthy little mitts on a copy of Playboy. Today, any twelve-year-old can walk up to a newsstand and buy himself a copy of FHM, Stuff, or Maxim and see pretty much the same thing, sans nipples, airbrushed pubic hair, and hand-me-down grossness.

Great Sex

Do you enjoy great sex? If so, you have porn to thank for it. Adult movies have undeniably improved the quality of our collective sex lives by showing us how they do things in the big leagues. Just like musicians draw inspiration by listening to other musicians, we draw inspiration by watching our porn counterparts at work. The net result? More satisfied customers.

know your classics

Well-rounded educations are rooted in the classics. After all, playwrights study Shakespeare, physicists study Newton, and Goths faithfully skim the liner notes of Morrissey albums past. Likewise, a student of smut has to be versed in the greats. But what makes a porno "great" in the first place? It's not just in the loins of the beholder. Generally speaking, all "classic porn" has to meet a few basic criteria:

★ It was produced between 1972 and 1984—widely considered to be the "Classic Era" of porno.
★ It was shot on film (as opposed to videotape).
★ It's free of implants, tattoos, and condoms.
★ It has some semblance of a plot.
★ Its stars have more hair than the floor of a barbershop.

Still, that leaves hundreds, maybe thousands, of movies to sift through. Where does one begin? Turn the page, dear reader . . .

A couple of things right off the bat: First, there are plenty of great pornos that didn't make this list. Yes, it's an outrage, but there's a very simple explanation—of the hundreds of classic pornos I've seen, these are my favorites. That's it. That's the scientific method. If I left yours off, or picked one that you can't stand—let me apologize in advance. You have only my terrible taste to blame.

Second, I don't love these films for the great sex. If you're looking for wall-to-wall grinding, you're looking in the wrong decades. In fact, the sex in many of these movies is, well, pretty awful. Nay, my friends of filth, I love these pornos because they wanted to be *more* than pornos. To give you an idea of my criteria:

★ **Ambition:** Does it aspire to be something more than run-of-the-mill?

★ **Directing:** Is there anything different about this? Am I entertained?

★ **Production Values:** How are the photography, music, sets, and costumes?

★ **Acting:** Is it better than the usual porn deadpan?

★ **Story:** Am I interested?

★ **Eroticism:** Finally, how's the sex?

I've also highlighted cast members, running times, and notable fetishes (if any of these are new to you, see chapter 4). So, without further ado, here are my top twenty favorites. No collection is complete without them. No life is complete without seeing them.

❶ The Opening of Misty Beethoven (VCA Pictures, 1976)

Without a doubt the best porno ever made. This "porno-fied" version of *Pygmalion* (or *My Fair Lady* if you prefer) took a year and a half to film on two continents, and contains some of the best dialogue, production values, and performances to ever grace the smutty screen. When we first meet the titular Misty, she's a Parisian streetwalker who scrapes by pleasuring elderly men in movie theaters. That changes when she's spotted by Seymour, a cosmopolitan sex expert played by the supremely talented Jamie Gillis. Seymour issues himself a challenge: Turn this lowly hooker into the next "Goldenrod Girl"—a spoof of *Playboy*'s Playmate of the Year. Misty's ensuing sexual and cultural education is both entertaining and erotic.

jamie gillis

constance money

With New York City and much of Europe serving as backdrop, she learns to satisfy one, then two, then three men at a time—all leading to her big unveiling in front of the world's sexual elite. While the acting is good across the board, it's Gillis who really shines here. His turn in *Misty* could hold its own in any mainstream Hollywood film (and earned him the Adult Film Association of America's Best Actor award). Legend holds that the film's cinematographer, Robert Rochester, is actually an Academy Award–winner working under an assumed name.

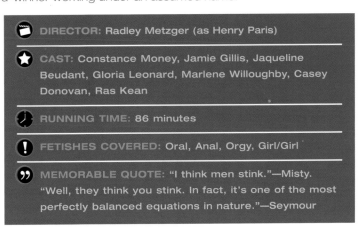

DIRECTOR: Radley Metzger (as Henry Paris)

CAST: Constance Money, Jamie Gillis, Jaqueline Beudant, Gloria Leonard, Marlene Willoughby, Casey Donovan, Ras Kean

RUNNING TIME: 86 minutes

FETISHES COVERED: Oral, Anal, Orgy, Girl/Girl

MEMORABLE QUOTE: "I think men stink."—Misty. "Well, they think you stink. In fact, it's one of the most perfectly balanced equations in nature."—Seymour

"**Brilliant new porn film. No other film is going to equal this one. It simply has to be the best film of 1976. 100%**"
—*Al Goldstein Midnight Blue*

"**A classic piece of erotica . . . it's the finest blue movie I've ever seen. Director Henry Paris keeps the action fast, fun and furious. It is inventive, opulent, and highly erotic.**"
—*Borden Scott, After Dark*

"The Opening of Misty Beethoven"

Introducing
Constance Money
with **Jamie Gillis Jaqueline Beudant**
Terri Hall/Gloria Leonard/Casey Donovan/Ras Kean
Directed by **Henry Paris**

A Quality Adult Film

2 The Dancers (VCX, 1981)

Crafted with skill, driven by a solid story, and featuring some unusually good acting, *The Dancers* has no business calling itself a porno—even though the premise sounds like standard fare: Four male strippers ("Jackie and the Dreams") roll into a small town to work the local nudie bar. During their stay, each of the men has a tryst with (at least) one of the locals. But that's where the clichés end. It's what happens when the clothes are on that sets *Dancers* apart. It includes what I consider the best scene ever filmed for an adult movie. It's a simple bit of dialogue between Richard Pacheco and Georgina Spelvin—so tenderly acted and directed that despite your best intentions, you find yourself getting emotional. Emotional? This is a porno! You're not supposed to use that box of tissues for tears! If you're someone who fast-forwards from sex scene to sex scene, you'll hate this film. Despise it, even. But if you're looking for a gentle introduction to the world of X-rated movies, do yourself a favor and check it out.

DIRECTOR: Anthony Spinelli

CAST: John Leslie, Georgina Spelvin, Richard Pacheco, Vanessa Del Rio, Joey Silvera, Kay Parker, Randy West

RUNNING TIME: 101 minutes

FETISHES COVERED: Interracial, Mature, Stripping, Adultery, Oral

MEMORABLE QUOTE: "I lost eighty points off my I.Q. A year later, the doctor told me I had to be a male stripper."—Joey

3 Taboo (Standard Digital, 1980)

Poor Barbara Scott (Kay Parker). Her no-good husband has run off with another woman, leaving her to raise their (unbelievably hunky) teenage son Paul by herself. Encouraged by friends, she dates a little—but it's no use. Each guy's a bigger jerk than the last. Oh, poor, poor Barbara Scott! Wherever is a sexless middle-aged woman to find true passion? A woman who lives alone with her (gorgeous, monstrously endowed, and constantly flirtatious) son? *Taboo* answered the age-old plea of "don't go there" with a resounding "oh, we're

DIRECTOR: Kirdy Stevens

CAST: Kay Parker, Mike Ranger, Dorothy LeMay, Juliet Anderson

RUNNING TIME: 85 minutes

FETISHES COVERED: Incest, Oral, Orgy, Facial, Girl/Girl, Masturbation, Older Woman/Younger Man

MEMORABLE QUOTE: "The minute they get it up, they let you down."—Gina going there, all right, and we're filming lots of close-ups, too." The film's legendary climax is one of the most famous (and steamiest) in all of porndom—a fact that Parker attributes to the off-screen attraction between her and costar Mike Ranger. The incestuous results spawned the biggest adult hit of the early 1980s (and more than ten sequels). Snappy dialogue and solid acting secure *Taboo* a permanent home at the top of every "totally gross but totally well-done" list.

4 Talk Dirty to Me (Dreamland, 1980)

Ever wonder what *Of Mice and Men* would've been like with penetration and a happier ending? (Seriously, am I the only one?) Regardless, anyone familiar with John Steinbeck's book will recognize the relationship between the smooth-talking babe magnet Jack (John Leslie) and his simpleton sidekick Lenny (Richard Pacheco). Flat broke, they wander San Francisco scamming free meals and trying to get laid. Jack spots Marlene (Jesie St. James)—gorgeous, rich, and sexually repressed—and issues himself a challenge: bed her down in three days or less. The rest is predictable enough— slowly but surely, Jack's charms thaw the ice queen, revealing her inner nymphomaniac.

Even Lenny gets a little dim-witted action by story's end. But as with most of director Anthony Spinelli's films, sex isn't the main appeal—it's the performances. They're far, far better than what porno calls for. *Dirty* was a huge box-office success and received the Adult Film Association of America's awards for Best Picture, Best Actor (Leslie), and Best Supporting Actor (Pacheco). Spinelli's nineteen-year-old son Mitchell helped pen the script—the first of their many father/son collaborations.

DIRECTOR: Anthony Spinelli

CAST: Jesie St. James, Juliet Anderson, Dorothy LeMay, John Leslie, Richard Pacheco

RUNNING TIME: 80 minutes

FETISHES COVERED: Three-Way, Girl/Girl, Masturbation, Older Woman/Younger Man, Voyeurism, Facial

MEMORABLE QUOTE: "A cookie for some nookie?"—Lenny

5 The Satisfiers of Alpha Blue (AVC, 1981)

"In the twenty-first century the world was perfect . . . almost." So begins Gerard Damiano's pessimistic vision of a future in which casual sex is forbidden (to control an exploding population). Everything from chicken to orgasms is offered in pill form, and women are chosen by lottery to be the birth mothers of test-tube babies. (One of the

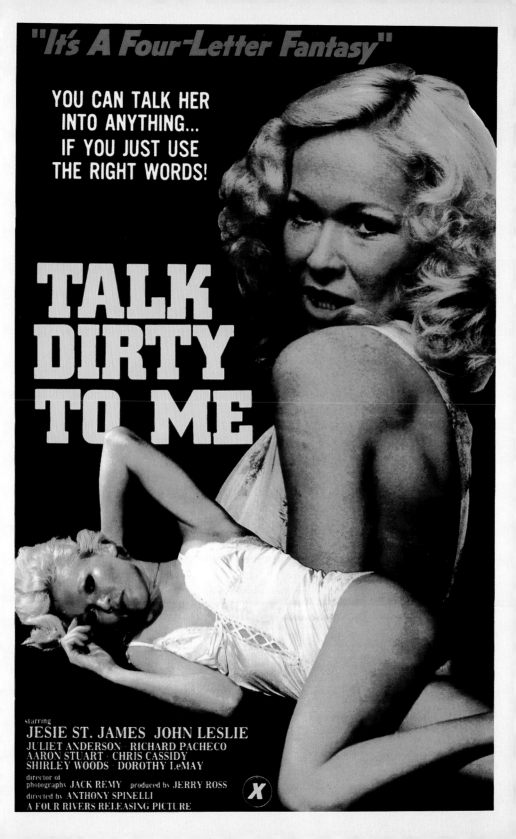

Gerard Damiano's

"The Satisfiers
of Alpha Blue"

ways *Alpha Blue* was ahead of its time: Women could genetically choose their baby's sex.) To get their rocks off, privileged citizens receive membership cards to Alpha Blue— a sort of sexual McDonald's. A hostess comes around, and customers order up "Satisfiers" (male or female) and sexual acts with numbers like "903" (sorry, you can't super-size that one). What's strange about *Alpha Blue* is that it's an *anti-porn* porno. Its

protagonist, Algon (Richard Bolla), ultimately realizes that sex without love is meaningless, and gives up his membership card. (I know what you're thinking—"Can I have it?") Sure, they could've spent a few more bucks on the sets, but the other production values are top-notch: stark, post-apocalyptic exteriors, superior photography, and one of the best musical scores in porn history.

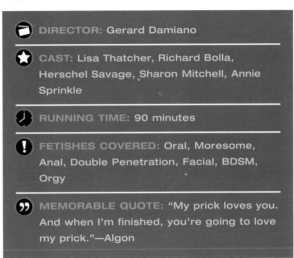

DIRECTOR: Gerard Damiano

CAST: Lisa Thatcher, Richard Bolla, Herschel Savage, Sharon Mitchell, Annie Sprinkle

RUNNING TIME: 90 minutes

FETISHES COVERED: Oral, Moresome, Anal, Double Penetration, Facial, BDSM, Orgy

MEMORABLE QUOTE: "My prick loves you. And when I'm finished, you're going to love my prick."—Algon

6 Insatiable (I-Candy, 1980)

Sandra Chase (Marilyn Chambers) seems to have everything a woman could ever hope for: youth and beauty, fortune and fame. She's even been cast in her first Hollywood film. Alas, there is one thing she never seems to have enough of . . . the

hot man-pole. At her estate in the English countryside, she fantasizes about past encounters and screws every costar in sight, but it's never enough. Out for a drive, she comes across a stranded motorist and ravages him, but the craving remains. The film ends with an extended dream sequence, in which Sandra imagines three lovers doing

DIRECTOR: Stu Segall (as Godfrey Daniels)

CAST: Marilyn Chambers, Jesie St. James, Serena, John Holmes, John Leslie, David Morris, Mike Ranger, Richard Pacheco

RUNNING TIME: 77 minutes

FETISHES COVERED: Anal, Facial, Girl/Girl, Moresome

MEMORABLE QUOTE: "I mean, Sandra Chase—famous model—is sucking on my pee-pee! Who's going to believe it?"—Artie

MARILYN CHAMBERS

is

Insatiable

Also Starring
SERENA · JOHN LESLIE · JESIE ST. JAMES
MIKE RANGER · DAVID MORRIS · RICHARD PACHECO
Featuring
JOHN C. HOLMES

Produced and Directed by
GODFREY DANIELS

Title song sung by
MARILYN CHAMBERS

A MIRACLE FILM Release

 NO ONE UNDER 18 ADMITTED

Color by EASTMAN KODAK

Anyone who's ever owned a porno knows how it feels to be a secret agent. The constant fear of having your cover blown. Of having to pull the shades before you make a move. Unless you live alone (and especially if you live with your parents), keeping your collection from falling into the wrong hands takes an effort worthy of the CIA. After conferring with some of my contacts in the world of international espionage, I can offer a couple of techniques that might very well save your (solo) sex life:

Stroke and Dagger

Covert Technique Alpha: "The Misleading Label" (VHS Viewers)

People are rarely suspicious of something left out in the open—a weakness you can exploit to throw them off the scent of your smut. Rather than hide your tapes at the bottom of the hamper, toss their original packaging and place them in new slipcovers. Label them with the least appealing titles you can imagine ("*Murder, She Wrote Marathon*," "C-SPAN2 Highlights"). Basically, think of the people you're trying to repel, then think of the last things they'd ever want to watch. Slide your porn somewhere between *Aladdin* and *Scarface* and enjoy!

Advantages: Allows your collection to be stored in plain sight. Also gives you the mischievous pleasure of watching people walk right by your porn, unaware.

Drawbacks: Works like a charm until your mother-in-law decides to kick back with a copy of "November 2004 Sales Presentation."

Covert Technique Bravo: "The Picture Frame" (DVD Viewers)

Simple steps to porn secrecy: Remove the disc from its case and slide it into a protective sleeve. Take one of those framed pictures off your wall and remove the backing. Place the DVD behind the picture and reassemble the frame. Hang it on the wall. Laugh like a comic book villain and marvel at your devious brilliance. (Word to the wise: Choose the picture carefully. If it's a picture of your grandmother, you'll never masturbate again).

Advantages: Barring earthquakes, your porn will never be found.

Drawbacks: Disassembling a picture frame every time you're in the mood.

everything they can to satisfy her (while background singers chant, "Sandra, suck it faster!"). Finally, the Wadd himself—John Holmes—appears. Surely he can satisfy the insatiable Sandra. But even after Holmes shoehorns his Cadillac into her "compacts only" parking space, she turns to the camera begging, "More . . . please . . . I need more!" A well-made film all around—no surprise when you consider that the film's director, Stu Segall, went on to mainstream success producing TV dramas like *Silk Stalkings*, *Renegade*, and *Pensacola: Wings of Gold*.

❼ Debbie Does Dallas (VCH, 1979)

If you were born after 1970, it was probably the first porno you could name. But that superbly catchy title is a bit misleading. Debbie, a virginal college cheerleader, is never actually *in* Dallas—but needs to get there in two weeks to cheer with the esteemed Texas Cowgirls. Alas, she doesn't have the money to go. In a touching display, the other girls on her squad prostitute themselves to raise the funds. Seems realistic enough. In fact, *Debbie* is full of good ol' American values: teamwork, industriousness, and sporting goods. And its effect on porn can still be felt today (just type "cheerleader" into any search engine and you'll see what I mean).

bam
woo

While making the film, the producers allegedly duped the State University of New York at Stony Brook into cooperating with the shoot (legend holds that some college officials even made cameos). Decent production values and unnervingly catchy music—not to mention the scene-stealing Georgette Sanders as Lisa—make this a must-have in any collection.

DIRECTOR: Jim Clark

CAST: Bambi Woods, Richard Balla, Robyn Byrd, Arcadia Lake, Georgette Sanders

RUNNING TIME: 72 minutes

FETISHES COVERED: Oral, Deep Throat, Facial, Three-Way, Older Man/Younger Woman, Masturbation, Interracial, Deflowering, Orgy

MEMORABLE QUOTE: "We should walk around the way we came into this world—stark naked."—Lisa

EVERYONE ON THE TEAM SCORES WHEN HER POM-POMS FLY!

DEBBIE DOES DALLAS

starring
BAMBI WOODS with
MISTY WINTER • PAT ALLURE • ROBYN BYRD • RIKKI O'NEAL
ARCADIA LAKE • PAULA HEAD • GEORGETTE SANDERS • RICHARD BALLA
Produced & Directed by JIM CLARK   Director of Photography BILLY BUDD
Written by MARIA MINESTRA   Production Supervisor DEXTER EAGLE

xXx

VIVID COLOR FOR LADIES AND GENTLEMEN OVER 21 YEARS

⑧ Alice in Wonderland (Cruiser Productions, 1976)

The first porno to have its own choreographer, *Alice in Wonderland* is an X-rated musical reimagining of Lewis Carroll's classic novel. In this version, Alice (Kristine DeBell) is a stunningly beautiful (and tragically prudish) young librarian who's constantly rejecting advances from her blue-balled boyfriend, William. In the movie's first song, Alice laments all the things she's missed in life: "Never played at patty-cake, kick the can, or caught a snake . . . " Then it's down the rabbit hole, where everyone from the Mad Hatter to the Queen of Hearts is waiting to give Alice lessons in loosening up. More song and dance numbers ensue (including my personal favorite, "What's a Nice Girl Like You Doing on a Knight Like This?"). Besides being a mega-budget (as pornos go) musical version of a children's book, *Alice* is unique in the fact that there's not a single penis in sight for the first twenty-five minutes of screen time. And while it may be more silly than sexy, you have to admire the fact that they pulled it off. By the way, Kristine DeBell went on to have a mainstream career in movies like *Meatballs* and TV pilots like *BJ and the Bear*—which, to my knowledge, was not about going down on hairy men.

🎬 DIRECTOR: Bud Townsend

⭐ CAST: Kristine DeBell, Alan Novak, Jerry Spelman

🕐 RUNNING TIME: 88 minutes

❗ FETISHES COVERED: Oral, Deflowering, Orgy, Girl/Girl, Interracial

💬 MEMORABLE QUOTE: "If it feels good, there's a good chance it must be bad."—Alice

BILL OSCO's...

Alice in Wonderland

an X-Rated Musical Comedy

STARRING PLAYBOY'S COVER GIRL — KRISTINE DE BELL

WITH LARRY GELMAN • ALLAN NOVAK • TERRY HALL • JASON WILLIAMS STAR OF *FLESH GORDON*

SCREENPLAY BY B. A. FREDRICKS

LYRICS AND MUSIC BY BUCKY SEARLES • ARRANGED AND CONDUCTED BY JACK STEARN & PETER MATZ

PRODUCED BY WILLIAM OSCO • DIRECTED BY BUD TOWNSEND

FROM THE PRODUCER OF *FLESH GORDON*

A GENERAL NATIONAL FILMS RELEASE

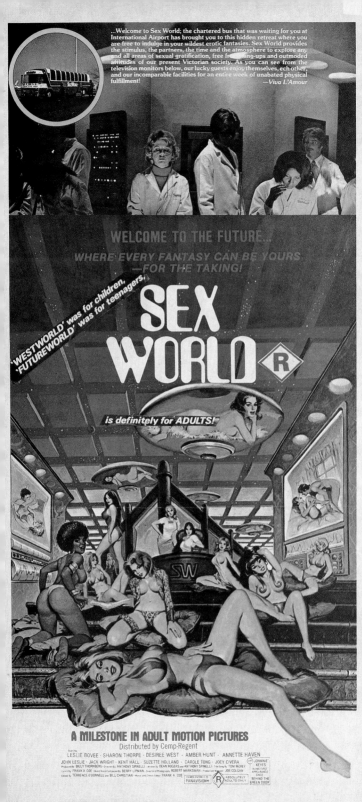

⑨ Sex World (Essex, 1978)

When porn icon Anthony Spinelli saw *Westworld* in 1973, he knew he'd found the perfect vehicle for a porno: A resort where people could live out their innermost desires without guilt or consequence—a place where humanoid robots catered to your every whim. Considered risky and expensive, it took over three years to secure financing. The result? A wildly witty and ambitious sci-fi porno with an all-star cast. *Sex World* follows a handful of people through their weekend at the resort, beginning with a bus trip to its secret location. Each has his or her own sexual hang-ups (which we see in flashback). Upon arrival, they're interviewed by technicians who determine the best remedies for their sexual ailments. The film plays out by showing us snippets of their varied, erotic encounters. To my knowledge, *Sex World* is the first porno to pay homage to *another* porno. One of the guests admits she's always wanted to be with Johnny Keyes—the infamous "Man in White" from *Behind the Green Door* (see #15). Does her fantasy come true? YOU'LL HAVE TO SEE FOR YOURSELF! All right, fine—it comes true.

DIRECTOR: Anthony Spinelli

CAST: Abigail Clayton, Annette Haven, Leslie Bovee, Amber Hunt, John Leslie, Joey Silvera, Kay Parker

RUNNING TIME: 90 minutes

FETISHES COVERED: Phone Sex, Facial, Masturbation, Interracial, Girl/Girl, Oral

MEMORABLE QUOTE: "I'll prove your spigot ain't no bigot!"—Black Girl

⑩ Deep Throat (Arrow, 1972)

Though it's technically inferior to most of the films on this list, *Deep Throat* remains important because it helped create the adult industry as we know it. In terms of box-office receipts and cultural significance, it was the *Star Wars*, *Titanic*, and *Harry Potter* of pornos. It's also the most profitable film of all time—shot for around $20,000, its earnings are estimated to be between

DIRECTOR: Gerard Damiano

CAST: Linda Lovelace, Harry Reems, Dolly Sharp, Carol Conners, Bob Phillips

RUNNING TIME: 61 minutes

FETISHES COVERED: Anal, Oral, Facial, Deep Throat, Smoking, Younger Woman/Older Man

MEMORABLE QUOTE: "Having a clitoris deep down at the bottom of your throat is better than having no clitoris at all."—Dr. Young

bill
harrison

linda
lovelace

$200 and $600 *million*. At its core, *Throat* is a moving story about overcoming a physical disability. We meet Linda, a lonely but attractive young woman who can't achieve an orgasm no matter how many partners or positions she tries. And believe me, she tries them all. Desperate, she seeks the advice of Dr. Young (Harry Reems), an unorthodox (i.e., unlicensed) specialist with a weakness for nurses and Groucho Marx one-liners. He examines Linda and (gasp!) finds the problem: a horrible birth defect has placed her clitoris in her throat! She's devastated, until the good doctor kindly introduces her to the world of "Deep Throat." At first, Linda turns out more gags than a magic shop, but after trying her new skills on a variety of Dr. Young's patients, she finally gets her big "O."

GERARD DAMIANO'S

DEEP
THROAT

HOW FAR DOES A GIRL HAVE TO GO TO UNTANGLE HER TINGLE?

EASTMANCOLOR Ⓧ ADULTS ONLY

IF
YOU LIKED
"DEEP THROAT"
AND
"SINGIN' IN THE RAIN"
YOU'RE GONNA
LOVE...

Blonde Ambition

...The First Adult Extravaganza!

The Amero Bros'. present SUZY MANDEL and DORY DEVON in "BLONDE AMBITION"
Also starring (in alphabetical order) Richard Bolla • Patricia Dale • Adam De Haven • Eric Edwards • Jamie Gillis
Jeanne Joseph • Molly Malone • Kurt Mann • David Morris • Wade Parker • George Payne & The Tara Belles
Screenplay by LaRue Watts   Produced and Directed by John and Lem Amero • In Color

11 Blonde Ambition (Video-X-Pix, 1980)

Now here's a porno that had me at "hello." When a stroke flick opens with a full-scale Broadway musical number, you know you're in for a good time—and from the first frame to the last, *Blonde Ambition* never stops one-upping itself. The movie follows the Kane sisters (Candy and Sugar, get it?) on their improbable rise to superstardom—a rise that begins in Coyote Fang, Wyoming. Their nightclub act is straight out of *Twin Peaks* (one sister tap dances while the other plays the tuba) but it's enough to impress Stephen (Eric Edwards)—a millionaire playboy who happens to be in the neighborhood. He invites the sisters to ride his private plane back to New York City, and after earning their mile-high cards, Candy (Dory Devon) and Sugar

wade parker

suzy mandel

(Suzy Mandel) start pounding the pavement. Their first gig is a hard-core remake of *Gone with the Wind*, produced by Miracle Pictures ("If it's a good picture . . . it's a Miracle!"), and complete with real peacocks (colored feathers glued to chickens). And things only get weirder—there's a sex scene on ice, a Concorde hijacking, a drag ball, and of course—singing and dancing! Packed with corny gags, *Blonde Ambition* is one of the only "fast-forward-proof" pornos ever made. As you'd expect, the production values are top-notch across the board.

DIRECTORS: John and Lem Amero

CAST: Dory Devon, Suzy Mandel, Richard Bolla, Eric Edwards

RUNNING TIME: 86 minutes

FETISHES COVERED: Oral, Bisexual Male, Masturbation, Threesome, Girl/Girl, Orgy

MEMORABLE QUOTE: "There's nothing like a riot in a fag bar and a night in the slammer to ensure showbiz immortality."—Narrator

Porn Theme for the Mainstream

It may seem like adult movies merely imitate their mainstream counterparts. But once in a while, inspiration flows the other way. Here are a few Hollywood flicks inspired by some of the biggest names and personalitites in all of porn:

Sex, Lies, and Videotape . . . (1989)

Steven Soderbergh's first feature may not deal directly with porn, but it's a thematic first cousin—full of adultery, voyeurism, and dirty talk. Graham (James Spader) is an impotent man whose only release comes through videotaping erotic conversations with women and pleasuring himself while watching them. Though these videotapes contain no actual penetration, they are in essence homemade pornography—their sole purpose is sexual arousal. A masterful look at the power sex holds over relationships.

The People vs. Larry Flynt (1996)

Directed by Milos Forman (*Amadeus*, *One Flew Over the Cuckoo's Nest*), *Flynt* is a thoroughly entertaining trip through the life of porn's most vehement defender. Though the real Flynt cooperated with the filmmakers, this is hardly a flattering self-portrait. From his youth in rural Kentucky to his multimillion-dollar publishing empire, he's portrayed (brilliantly, by Woody Harrelson) as a reluctant hero—a huckster who only stands up for free speech after the loss of it threatens his own livelihood.

Boogie Nights (1997)

It doesn't get any better than this. Paul Thomas Anderson's homage to porn's golden age faithfully recreates the industry as it was in the 1970s and early '80s. The décor is perfect. The spoofs of classic pornos are dead-on. Even the characters are rooted in real legends: The shy yet hung-like-an-elephant Dirk Diggler (Mark Wahlberg) is a tribute to John Holmes. The old-time director Jack Horner (Burt Reynolds), who struggles to change with the business, is an amalgamation of Anthony Spinelli, Jamie Gillis, and others. Required viewing for any fan of classic porn.

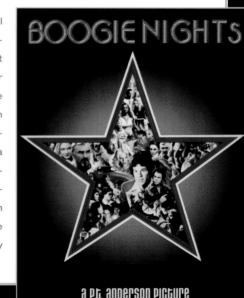

BOOGIE NIGHTS

a p.t. anderson picture

Rated X (2000)

This mediocre effort focuses on a time when San Francisco was the center of the porn universe. Emilio Estevez and Charlie Sheen star as Jim and Artie Mitchell, the brothers who made Marilyn Chambers a household name with *Behind the Green Door*. The Mitchell brothers eventually spiraled into drug addiction and bankruptcy, a descent that ended when Jim shot and killed Artie in 1991. If you're interested in porno history, it's worth a look.

Wonderland (2003)

In 1981, two men and two women were found bludgeoned to death at 8763 Wonderland Avenue in the Hollywood Hills. Though it remains uncertain, one of the accomplices was rumored to be porn legend John Holmes. Directed by the (aptly named) James Cox, the film recreates the murders from different points of view while painting a portrait of Holmes's decline—his drug dealing, growing addiction to cocaine, and estrangement from his still-caring wife. *Wonderland's* DVD includes the excellent documentary *Wadd: The Life and Times of John C. Holmes*.

A Dirty Shame (2004)

I was tempted to write "Any John Waters Movie," since you can count on a fetish or two in most of his work—from the foot-obsessed "Baltimore Stomper" in *Polyester* (1981) to the gay bar that forbids tea-bagging in *Pecker* (1998). In *Shame*, Tracey Ullman plays a sexually repressed housewife who keeps her daughter locked away (for constantly exposing her "criminally enlarged" breasts). But after suffering a concussion, she develops an insatiable sexual appetite. It's a plot twist as old as porno itself—the uptight woman finally realizes what she's been missing and goes on a hump-a-thon.

HUSTLER's HIGHEST RATING!

That unrelenting desire to release those inner longings that are universal and timeless...

Babylon Pink

The Unexpected Pleasures Of Seven Ladies

Starring
SAMANTHA FOX
VANESSA DEL RIO
ARCADIA BLUE
Introducing
DEBBIE REVENGE · MERLE MICHAELS and
GEORGETTE SAUNDERS as the teenager
With BOBBY ASTYR · RICHARD BOLLA
ERIC EDWARDS · DAVID MORRIS · DAVE RUBY and
GEORGINA SPELVIN
Produced by CECIL HOWARD
Written and Directed by HENRI PACHARD
A WinVan Production

12 Babylon Pink (Command, 1979)

Winner of the 1979 Adult Film Association of America award for Best Picture, *Pink* bills itself as a film told through the fantasies of several interconnected New York women. That's *almost* true. They're actually the fantasies men desperately *want* women to have (I mean, let's be honest—the film was produced by, directed by, and marketed to guys). There's the overbearing boss who dreams of being dominated by her male underling. The shy virgin who fantasizes of a tryst with her uncle. The bored housewife who imagines sampling the produce of her neighborhood grocer. Still, you can't ignore the fact that *Babylon Pink* is an exceptional piece of porno. Shot on 35mm film, the first thing you notice is how good the movie looks. The exteriors are a time capsule of New York City in the late '70s and worth the price of admission alone. The best sex scenes belong to Vanessa Del Rio and the virginal Georgette Sanders, who made only six films in her short career. For shame, Georgette!

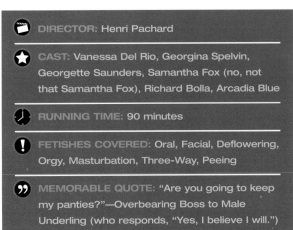

DIRECTOR: Henri Pachard

CAST: Vanessa Del Rio, Georgina Spelvin, Georgette Saunders, Samantha Fox (no, not that Samantha Fox), Richard Bolla, Arcadia Blue

RUNNING TIME: 90 minutes

FETISHES COVERED: Oral, Facial, Deflowering, Orgy, Masturbation, Three-Way, Peeing

MEMORABLE QUOTE: "Are you going to keep my panties?"—Overbearing Boss to Male Underling (who responds, "Yes, I believe I will.")

13 Wanda Whips Wall Street (Video-X-Pix, 1981)

Years before Oliver Stone made Wall Street synonymous with greed, it was known as a bastion of sexual depravity; a place where people traded more venereal diseases than shares. That is, if you believe the story of Wanda Brandt (Veronica Hart)—a young go-getter who ditches small-town America for a shot at the Big Apple. After landing at one of the biggest firms in the city—a brokerage that emphasizes

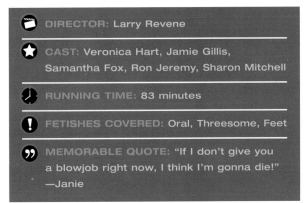

DIRECTOR: Larry Revene

CAST: Veronica Hart, Jamie Gillis, Samantha Fox, Ron Jeremy, Sharon Mitchell

RUNNING TIME: 83 minutes

FETISHES COVERED: Oral, Threesome, Feet

MEMORABLE QUOTE: "If I don't give you a blowjob right now, I think I'm gonna die!" —Janie

WHEN WANDA TALKS — EVERYBODY LISTENS!

WANDA WHIPS WALL STREET

"porking" over "pork bellies"—Wanda wastes no time climbing the corporate ladder. Her strategy? Simple. Bang an executive, and then blackmail him into signing over his shares of the firm. As she gobbles up shares (and then some), Wanda's boss becomes suspicious, and hires a detective to get to the "bottom" of his company's declining value. And boy, does he ever. Again, and again, and again. *Wanda Whips Wall Street* is basically *Working Girl* without all the bothersome clothing. The fast, shtick-heavy script is complemented by top-notch photography, sets, and locations (some scenes even use the real NYSE as a backdrop).

⑭ Every Inch a Lady (Video-X-Pix, 1975)

Deviations, Inc., has what you're looking for. No matter how freaky the fetish, or how outlandish the request, if you've got the cash, they'll make it happen. Lovers Crystal (Darby Lloyd Rains) and Chico (Harry Reems) run this sex empire

from their penthouse apartment in Manhattan. But things weren't always so good. Until a few years ago, they were common street hustlers constantly getting pinched by the fuzz. That is, until they joined forces and started a "legitimate" escort service. But now, someone within the organization is plotting a coup! Will our heroes discover the scheme before it's too late? Can Crystal resist the advances of her lesbian secretary? Do you honestly give a shit? I couldn't help comparing this movie to the real life drama in its stars' lives. See, *Lady* was made shortly after *Deep Throat* whipped the country into a tizzy. During that period,

people like Reems were threatened with jail for appearing in porn. And just like his character, he eventually proved that success was the best revenge. Am I reading into this too much? Probably. Still, *Lady* is fast, funny, and well made. Plus, you get to see Reems shove a carrot up Jamie Gillis's ass—and for a veggiephile like me, that's like Christmas morning, baby.

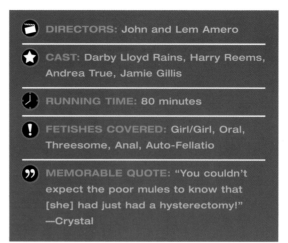

DIRECTORS: John and Lem Amero

CAST: Darby Lloyd Rains, Harry Reems, Andrea True, Jamie Gillis

RUNNING TIME: 80 minutes

FETISHES COVERED: Girl/Girl, Oral, Threesome, Anal, Auto-Fellatio

MEMORABLE QUOTE: "You couldn't expect the poor mules to know that [she] had just had a hysterectomy!" —Crystal

⑮ Behind the Green Door (Mitchell Brothers, 1972)

Released the same year as *Deep Throat*, the controversy surrounding *Green Door* was centered on its star, Marilyn Chambers. Here was the typical all-American girl—the wholesomely pretty, petite face of the detergent Ivory Snow—having hard-core sex on film. Chambers (who doesn't speak a word of dialogue in the entire movie) plays Gloria, a lone traveler who checks into a quiet resort. But there are shadowy figures watching her from the moment she arrives, and it isn't long before she's kidnapped and taken to an underground "sex club." Meanwhile, a black-tie audience gathers in the adjacent theater. Gloria, now thoroughly frightened and confused, is led (through a green door) onto the stage. From this point, the film plays out very much like a documentary: Gloria is forced to have various sexual experiences on stage as some of the audience members pleasure themselves. Of course, her fear and resistance soon give way to acceptance and ecstasy (this is still a porno, after all).

DIRECTORS: Jim and Artie Mitchell

CAST: Marilyn Chambers, Johnny Keyes

RUNNING TIME: 68 minutes

FETISHES COVERED: Deflowering, Interracial, Moresome, Girl/Girl, Trapeze, Orgy

MEMORABLE QUOTE: "Your calves— try to think of them as part of your feet."—Lisa

The Mitchell Brothers Present

the all·American girl

MARILYN CHAMBERS in

Behind the Green Door

Ⓧ   adults only

mitchell brothers film group/san francisco

16 Tell Them Johnny Wadd Is Here (Arrow, 1975)

My favorite of Holmes's Johnny Wadd series, *Tell Them* would barely qualify as pornography by today's standards. The sex scenes are relatively limp and separated by long patches of dialogue. There are endless montages of Holmes driving and walking on the beach. One sequence of Holmes loading his gun plays out for two minutes and thirteen seconds. Shot on location in Mexico (a whole three hours' drive from Los Angeles), *Tell Them* sends the studly detective South of the Border to help his old buddy Sam (Tyler Moore). Sam's run afoul of a local drug runner, who—cue organ music—also happens to be married to Wadd's ex-wife! Okay, so if it's not the plot, and it's not the sex, why is it a "must-see?" The Wadd, baby—that's why. John Holmes. It's his earnestness

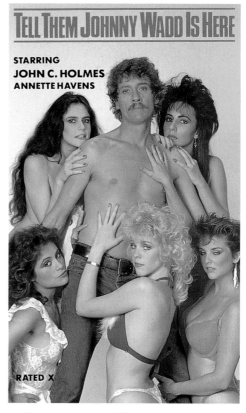

TELL THEM JOHNNY WADD IS HERE

STARRING
JOHN C. HOLMES
ANNETTE HAVENS

RATED X

and his total commitment to every line of dialogue, every fake punch, and every steely-eyed stare. Add some unintentionally hilarious fight sequences (hilariously parodied in *Boogie Nights*), and you've got the perfect porno to laugh with. It's also a record of Holmes in his prime, before drugs and disease wasted him away. If you can't get enough of the Wadd, check out *Liquid Lips* (1976).

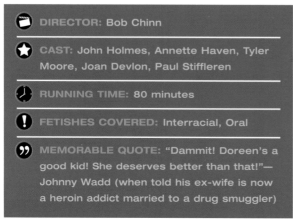

DIRECTOR: Bob Chinn

CAST: John Holmes, Annette Haven, Tyler Moore, Joan Devlon, Paul Stiffleren

RUNNING TIME: 80 minutes

FETISHES COVERED: Interracial, Oral

MEMORABLE QUOTE: "Dammit! Doreen's a good kid! She deserves better than that!"—Johnny Wadd (when told his ex-wife is now a heroin addict married to a drug smuggler)

⑰ Female Athletes (Video-X-Pix, 1977)

Here's a message for young ladies everywhere: You can be anything you endeavor to be; achieve any goal; realize any dream—as long as you're also an unabashed whore. Or at least that's the message of *Female Athletes*, which opens by recapping the advances in women's liberation—ironic, seeing that it's about to set that movement back a few centuries. Annette Haven plays Linda, secretary and full-time penis receptacle to the editor of a failing sports rag. She has some ideas that could save the magazine, but nobody's listening. Why? Because she's a silly *woman*, that's why! But finally, after increasing her boss's circulation, she gets a shot at doing the same for the magazine. Linda adopts a new format that celebrates (i.e., exploits the scrumptious bodies of) female athletes. Sales skyrocket, and Linda's promoted to editor, where she conducts herself with the utmost pro-fessionalism—forcing the mail-room boy to eat her out every day and marrying her former boss (the same guy who dis-missed her as a dingbat). And his wedding gift to her? An orgy, where she's mercilessly gangbanged! Let's hear it for equality!

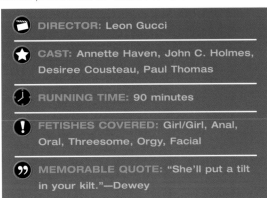

DIRECTOR: Leon Gucci

CAST: Annette Haven, John C. Holmes, Desiree Cousteau, Paul Thomas

RUNNING TIME: 90 minutes

FETISHES COVERED: Girl/Girl, Anal, Oral, Threesome, Orgy, Facial

MEMORABLE QUOTE: "She'll put a tilt in your kilt."—Dewey

⑱ The Bite (VCX, 1975)

If you felt *The Sting* was sorely lacking full-frontal nudity, you're in for a treat. Set in the throes of the Great Depression, *The Bite* is a funny, faithful parody of the classic Newman/Redford film. Three grifters—Sweet Kate, The Toledo Kid, and Johnny Memphis—decide to get in bed with each other (in every possi-ble sense) and swindle a local banker named Francis B. Dobbs. The cons set up a phony brothel, complete with call girls and customers (sen-ators, governors . . . hey, just

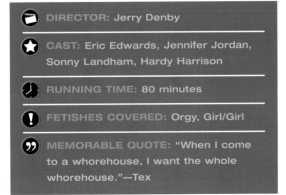

DIRECTOR: Jerry Denby

CAST: Eric Edwards, Jennifer Jordan, Sonny Landham, Hardy Harrison

RUNNING TIME: 80 minutes

FETISHES COVERED: Orgy, Girl/Girl

MEMORABLE QUOTE: "When I come to a whorehouse, I want the whole whorehouse."—Tex

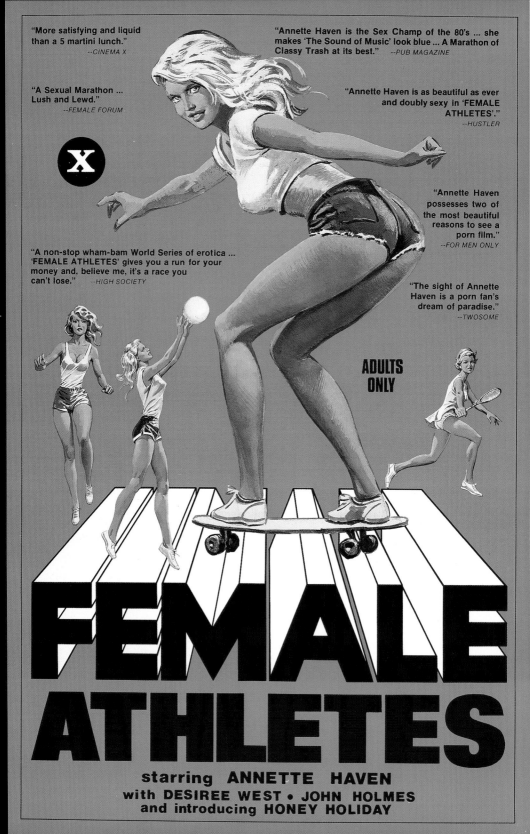

X

ADULTS ONLY

FEMALE ATHLETES

starring ANNETTE HAVEN
with DESIREE WEST • JOHN HOLMES
and introducing HONEY HOLIDAY

The Bite

... It Puts A Big Sting Into Sex

(TĪGRIS), FEMALE OF THE SPECIES... FOREVER ON THE PROWL!

Tigresses

...and other man~eaters

the tigresses...

**VANESSA DEL RIO   JACK & JILL MONROE
SAMANTHA FOX   RIKKI O'NEAL   The SLOAN TWINS**

like real life!). At first Dobbs doesn't approve of this "house of ill repute." But once he sees how much money they're raking in, he jumps at the chance to invest. Like *The Sting*, there's a twist or two at the end. A word to the horny: *The Bite* is full of jokes, fast-paced montages, and decent filmmaking. It is *not*, however, full of hard-core action.

⑲ Tigresses . . . and Other Man-Eaters (Video-X-Pix, 1979)

There are certain movies that ask the audience to buy into a premise. For instance, if you don't believe that a giant gorilla can fall for a five-foot blonde, you're not going to enjoy *King Kong*. The same is true for *Tigresses*, which begins by asking us to accept this self-evident truth: That all women are created equally horny and lose all semblance of self-control when they see pubes. That they are, well . . . *Tigresses*—hunting genitals like a tiger hunts its prey. (Luckily, I had no problem accepting this premise). Our narrator (Samantha Fox) splits her time between giving head and setting up each of the four vignettes that make up the film. First there's Holly, the athlete who beats men at sports, then beats them some more. Next up is Jill, who casts her net at the pier in hopes of roping a longshoreman. Then there's Naomi and Nancy—identical twins who must have one helluva narcissistic streak, since they can't keep their hands off each other. Finally, there's Rosita (Vanessa Del Rio)—a South American businesswoman who "no speaka the English" and likes to close big deals back at her place. *Tigresses* takes the "more is more" approach—more scenes, more stars, more acts of unspeakable wantonness.

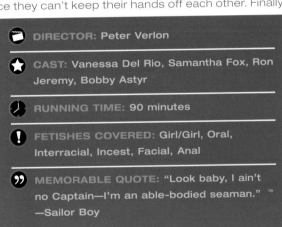

DIRECTOR: Peter Verlon

CAST: Vanessa Del Rio, Samantha Fox, Ron Jeremy, Bobby Astyr

RUNNING TIME: 90 minutes

FETISHES COVERED: Girl/Girl, Oral, Interracial, Incest, Facial, Anal

MEMORABLE QUOTE: "Look baby, I ain't no Captain—I'm an able-bodied seaman." —Sailor Boy

⓴ Deep Inside Annie Sprinkle (Video-X-Pix, 1981)

Take a deep breath before you press play, because this movie has the most disturbing opening in the history of porn. Smut queen Annie Sprinkle plays a few notes on a grand piano, looks directly into the lens, and greets the audience. So far, so good, right? But then, out of nowhere, she presents a collection of photos—*actual* photos—from her childhood. There's Annie as a baby; Annie at sweet sixteen—and Annie at age five (and "still a virgin," she's compelled to add). Annie "My real name is Ellen . . . don't tell anybody" even shares a family portrait, and mentions her parents' struggles accepting her porn career. Can you *imagine* walking into a theater to get your rocks off, only to find yourself taking an inventory of the star-

annie sprinkle

let's real-life problems? Is there a more effective cure for the common hard on? Maybe not, but on some levels, it's also ingenious. By making herself a "real person," there's added naughtiness to watching Annie violate Ron Jeremy's rectum, or pee on a lover's stomach (she ain't called "Sprinkle" for nothing, folks). After

those first few minutes of self-revelation, the rest of the film plays out as a fragmented series of encounters showcasing Annie's many talents. And though it's not the best-*looking* porno ever made, its groundbreaking opening makes *Deep Inside* required viewing.

DIRECTOR: Ellen Steinberg (as Annie Sprinkle)

CAST: Annie Sprinkle, Sassy, Ron Jeremy

RUNNING TIME: 97 min

FETISHES COVERED: Girl/Girl, Anal, Moresome, Squirting, Masturbation, Rimming, Oral

MEMORABLE QUOTE: "I got nailed by the carpenters, I got laid by the carpet layers, and I got real turned on by the electricians."—Annie

THE GOLDEN GIRL OF PORN!

XXX

Deep Inside Annie Sprinkle

☆ 5 modern classics

Most of today's pornos have the artistic content of a septic tank, but there are exceptions. A handful of contemporary films cling to the notion that pornos can be erotic *and* entertaining at the same time. They aspire to create bigger, better, more creative smut—complete with plots and production values. And while they don't always succeed, you have to give them credit for trying. Here are five of the best.

1 Loaded (Digital Playground, 2004)

Gunfights, car chases, stunts, helicopter shots, nightvision rifles, digital effects, explosions, and flamethrowers. Not what you'd expect from a porno. This huge-for-a-porn-budget homage to *Bad Boys* and *Lethal Weapon* leaves no cliché unturned, starting with the good cop/bad cop partnership: Detective Simms (Eric Masterson) is the "by the book" family man with problems at home. His partner, Roth (Barrett Blake), is the chain-smoking loose cannon that no one else will work with. Their sexy lieutenant is constantly threatening to revoke their badges whenever their "shoot first, don't ask questions" methods leave half the city in ruins. *Loaded*'s plot picks up when sexy young Heather (Jesse Jane) watches in horror as a crime boss executes her boyfriend. After a pair of narrow escapes, she winds up in protective custody with Simms and Roth. Perhaps aroused by their constant stream of witty banter, she bones one of them in a matter of hours. The rest writes itself: They bring Heather on a stakeout, which leads to a shootout, which leads to her kidnapping. Simms and Roth get kicked off the force—that is, until Roth

"convinces" the lieutenant to give them one more chance. They mount a daring rescue, kill tons of bad guys, rescue the girl, and waste the crime boss. Writer/director/editor Nic Andrews (see page 125) keeps the pace up with a blaring hip-hop soundtrack and caffeinated editing style. You won't find a contemporary porno with bigger ambitions or better production values.

DIRECTOR: Nic Andrews

CAST: Jesse Jane, Barrett Blade, Eric Masterson, Tyce Bune, Brittney Skye, Cheyne Collins, Asia Carrera, Lea De Mae, Lee Stone, Chris Webber

RUNNING TIME: 90 minutes

FETISHES COVERED: Facial, Oral, Adultery

MEMORABLE QUOTE: "I can't leave her here! She might start fucking the toilet plunger, or the guy at the front desk." —Detective Roth

2 Les Vampyres (Cal Vista, 2000)

They're hot, they're horny, and they want to suck you dry—in every possible way. Klint (Joel Lawrence) and Jenny (Jewel Valmont) are your average sexually charged couple driving up California's coast for a weekend getaway. But things take a turn for the weird when they meet a trio of attractive, sophisticated women at their hotel. One of them—Veronika (Syren)—seems strangely obsessed with Jenny. Klint is suspicious, and rightly so. For these women are vampires (we know this because we've seen them seduce men, screw them, and then suck the blood out of their penises). Meanwhile, Jenny is having terrible nightmares—flashbacks to some

centuries-old castle. Naturally, it turns out that Jenny is actually a reincarnated bloodsucker who's finally found her old star-crossed lover, Veronika. After reclaiming her place at the top of the food chain, she and the other vamps get rid of some dead weight (Klint) and fly off into the moonrise. *Vampyres* is dark and stylish, with unusual attention to detail, top-notch photography, and Ron Jeremy in his greatest cameo (blink and you'll miss it). Director James Avalon (see page 124) gets some remarkably decent performances out of his actors, especially Syren.

DIRECTOR: James Avalon

CAST: Syren, Jewel Valmont, Joel Lawrence, Wendi Knight, Brick Majors, Violet Love, Jack Hammer, Samantha, Brandon Irons, Nick Orleans

RUNNING TIME: 90 minutes

FETISHES COVERED: Oral, Anal, Girl/Girl, Three-Way, Facial, Masturbation, Adultery

MEMORABLE QUOTE: "C'mon, big boy, put down the cross. I'm not into that kinky stuff."—Vampire Hooker

3 Misty Beethoven: The Musical (VCA, 2004)

sunset thomas

"Don't want to piss on you in an alley, don't want you puking on my ass. I said, baby, baby, please—I want a little class." So sings Darren Daly as he gets a blowjob in the opening number of this all-new *Misty*. Unlike the original, *The Musical* focuses on the super-wealthy, super-horny Daly, who's become bored with sex. Sure, there's always a maid standing by to fellate him at a moment's notice, but he requires a challenge—something new. Darren's penis suddenly bursts into its own musical number (yes, you read that correctly), during which the audience is encouraged to "follow the bouncing balls" at the bottom of the screen—reason enough to rent this one. He goes "slumming" in a sex club where he meets a reluctant prostitute named, of course, Misty Beethoven. Like the original classic, the goal is to transform her from common street trash to cosmo-politan sex goddess. Misty trains and trains. She practices her oral skills on a trio of singing butlers, studies porn tapes, and jets off to Europe to screw strangers. But this is a musical, and what Misty *really* wants to do is sing. And sing she does—so well, in fact, that she's able to leave Darren's sexual experiment for a music career. Predictably, her big concert turns into an onstage bone-a-thon and rousing finale. Sure, it's no *Chicago*, but come on—there's a singing *dick* in it.

DIRECTOR: Veronica Hart

CAST: Sunset Thomas, Randy Spears, Chloe, Julie Meadows, Evan Stone, Asia Carrera, Kelly Steele, Michelle Lay, F. J. Lincoln

RUNNING TIME: 120 minutes

FETISHES COVERED: Oral, Anal, Facial, Moresome, Girl/Girl, Interracial

MEMORABLE QUOTE: "Eight bucks says you'll lick my ass till it's nice and shiny."—Sex Club Patron

4 Sex Angels (Private, 2004)

They fight ninjas, they ski, they defuse bombs, and they have an insatiable thirst for baby batter. What else would you expect from the porn versions of *Charlie's Angels*? In fact, every moment that isn't spent saving the world is spent between the sheets. What's the movie about? Who knows? Just like its Hollywood counterpart, *Sex Angels'* plot is held together by chewing gum and loose bits of string. Someone with a bomb wants to destroy the world. The Angels (Mya Diamond, Jennifer Dark, and Sandy Style) have to find it before it's too blah, blah, blah. What really matters are the skimpy costumes and settings. There's a ninja training facility's locker room. A lesbian bar in the Alps. Most of all, there's the sex. It's first-rate, making up for some sloppy production values (you can frequently hear the director barking orders in the background). *Angels'* other saving grace is its willingness to be silly, like when one of the girls has a flashback of her master's sage advice (see quote below).

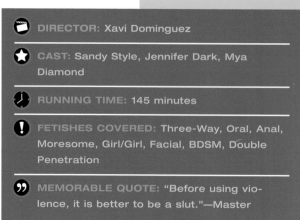

DIRECTOR: Xavi Dominguez

CAST: Sandy Style, Jennifer Dark, Mya Diamond

RUNNING TIME: 145 minutes

FETISHES COVERED: Three-Way, Oral, Anal, Moresome, Girl/Girl, Facial, BDSM, Double Penetration

MEMORABLE QUOTE: "Before using violence, it is better to be a slut."—Master

5 Repo Girl (Digital Playground, 2003)

We meet Claire (Celeste)—a convicted car thief—on the day she's released from prison. She goes to see her parole officer, who's in the habit of "cutting deals" with the female convicts. When Claire refuses to put out, he lays down the hard truth: she has forty-eight hours to get a job, or it's back to the big house. Before dusting off her résumé, Claire visits her comically trailer-trashy mother and stepfather. But it isn't long before "daddy" puts the moves on, and she leaves in disgust. A flyer leads her to a repossession company (staffed by people who wear tweed jackets and neckties over their T-shirts). Claire is told she can have a job as a "Repo Girl" if she can pass the age-old test: repossess three cars in eight hours. With the clock ticking, she sets off on her mission. Each repo leads to something sexually bizarre, like the scene-stealing Penny as "Schizo Girl"—a prudish bookworm who argues with her two alternate personalities (a drunk wearing a top hat and a nympho in a fur coat). Does Claire get the job? Of course she does—it's not the plot that makes this a classic. *Repo Girl* is a refreshingly stupid throwback to porn's classic comedies. It never takes itself seriously, and more importantly, it never bores. If you get your hands on the DVD, don't miss the "behind the scenes" segment, which may be funnier than the film itself.

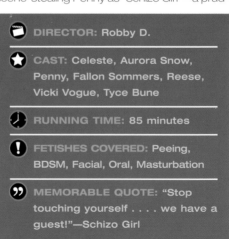

DIRECTOR: Robby D.

CAST: Celeste, Aurora Snow, Penny, Fallon Sommers, Reese, Vicki Vogue, Tyce Bune

RUNNING TIME: 85 minutes

FETISHES COVERED: Peeing, BDSM, Facial, Oral, Masturbation

MEMORABLE QUOTE: "Stop touching yourself . . . . we have a guest!"—Schizo Girl

There are two classic pornos I've come to love, but couldn't in good conscience call them "classics." Recommending them without a warning would be like going to college and majoring in philosophy—it's tempting, but stupid and irresponsible. In my opinion, these are both "must-see" movies. They're just a little . . . different. Consider yourself warned.

① Let My Puppets Come (Caballero, 1976)

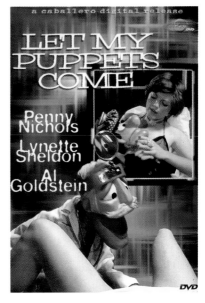

Puppet semen shooting out of a puppet penis. Funny? Or sign of the apocalypse? I'm still not sure, but I do know this—by far the weirdest thing about *Let My Puppets Come* is that it exists. That acclaimed porn director Gerard Damiano (*Deep Throat*, *The Devil in Miss Jones*) and a band of professionals actually MADE A PUPPET PORNO. The plot: Businessmen Ned, Fred, and Red need to come up with some cash—*quick*. The dreaded Mr. Big is threatening to break their felt-covered legs if he doesn't get his money. Solution? Make a porno, of course! There's the puppet dog going down on the puppet girl (not to worry, his shots are up to date). The puppet nurse going down on the puppet patient. And, yes, the puppet/human sex. There are also commercials for Lusterine mouthwash and Climax Watches ("Isn't it time you had a climax?"). I know it's stupid. I know it's wrong. And yet I watch, wondering, "Why aren't my eyeballs bursting into flames?" If you were planning on spending the weekend sniffing glue, do your body a favor—rent this instead.

🎬 **DIRECTOR:** Gerard Damiano

⭐ **CAST:** Puppets, Penny Nichols, Lynette Sheldon, Al Goldstein

🕐 **RUNNING TIME:** 45 minutes

❗ **FETISHES COVERED:** Felt, Puppet/Puppet, Puppet/Human, Puppet Oral, Puppet Bestiality

💬 **MEMORABLE QUOTE:** "I'm sorry, he's having a heart attack right now. May I take a message?"—Miss Bliss

② Kate and the Indians (TVX, 1980)

You haven't lived until you've seen a Nazi dwarf getting a blowjob from an Indian. Like the birth of your first child, it has a way of bringing your life into focus—of making everything else seem insignificant. *Indians* follows the bumbling Professor Von Martin (Jack Shute) and his hot young apprentice Kate (Kandi Barbour) on an expedition in the Southern California desert—a desert teeming with Indians (apparently unaware that it's 1980). But these aren't just any Indians—they're a collection of offensive stereotypes *dressed* as Indians! Like Moonbeam the Medicine Man, a tall, jive-talking black man who loves watermelon. And Limpin' Lip, his white, toga-clad brother who loves being gay. And yes, a dwarf (named Little Big Man) who wears a Nazi helmet. Kate and the Professor are kidnapped and forced to partici-

DIRECTOR: Allen Swift

CAST: Kay Parker, Kandi Barbour, Mike Ranger, Louie Short Stud

RUNNING TIME: 83 minutes

FETISHES COVERED: Girl/Girl, Orgy, Facial, Oral

MEMORABLE QUOTE: "I've kissed a cockatoo."—Limpin' Lip

pate in tribal sex rituals. As for the rest of the story—do you really care? *Indians* is the *Airplane!* of porn—it doesn't have a serious bone in its body, and it always goes for the cheap shot. Its fast-motion chases are straight out of *Benny Hill*, and its dialogue is straight out of fourth grade. Finally, a porno I can relate to!

FACT: Porn VHS cassettes and DVDs get more wear and tear than the rest of your collection. They also cost four to five times more than mainstream releases. Therefore, it behooves you to treat those little darlings with tender loving care. At no extra cost, here are a few ways to keep the good times rolling for years to come.

DVD

Contrary to what we all thought in 1997, DVDs (like CDs) degrade over time. Sure, they're smaller, crisper, and cooler, but they're also easier to destroy than a good old videotape.

Handling: Never, ever, ever touch the playing surface of a DVD. If you haven't learned that by now, there's no helping you.

Cleaning: Using a lint-free cloth (not a paper towel), wipe in straight lines from the center of the disc to the outer edge. *Don't* wipe in little circles. If you do, God will know. Also: Don't use CD-cleaning devices or chemicals—they may not be safe for your DVDs.

Storage: Never leave your DVDs in direct sunlight, or they'll end up looking like the clocks from Salvador Dali's *The Persistence of Memory*—a painting worth millions of dollars. Worth of your heat-warped porn? NOTHING.

Always wipe in straight lines from center of the disc to the outer edge.

VHS

Some of these faithful old friends may be getting on in years, but that's no reason to toss them in the wastebasket.

Handling: I don't care how hot that frame is—don't leave your tapes paused for minutes at a time! It puts wear on the tape *and* the VCR. Also: If you put a cold tape into a warm VCR, tiny water droplets could form inside the machine and effectively pop a cap in your tape's ass. So remember—*never* store your porn in the refrigerator.

Cleaning: Your greatest ally in the fight against dirty tapes is canned air. Never touch the precious magnetic tape—just use a few well-aimed puffs to keep dust and dirt from building up. And to ensure crystal-clear penetration close-ups, use a head-cleaning tape in your VCR about once a month.

Storage: As with DVDs, direct sunlight is the enemy. But VHS tapes have another Achilles' heel: magnetic fields. Placing tapes on top of your TV, stereo speakers, or anything with a magnet inside could lead to unwanted loss of porn. Also: Keep those slipcovers on! If there's dust on your tape, then there's dust in your VCR. And if there's dust in your VCR, you might as well crawl into a hole and die.

the pantheon of porn

Many came (and came, and came) and went—few left more than a stain or two. The classic era saw thousands of new porn faces (and other body parts) pass before the lens, most of which vanished into the ether of postcoital obscurity. But a handful of special performers managed to transcend the label of "porn actor" and become something more than the sum of their movies. They're the names and faces (and other body parts) any self-respecting pornophile needs to know . . .

Today, most porn starlets are judged by the size of their implants, their number of tattoos, and their willingness to test the elasticity of their orifices. But the ladies of classic porn were different. They came from a time when sexuality and talent counted just as much as looks. When you weren't considered a "has-been" at nineteen (some didn't even start *making* pornos until their forties). They looked like women you might see at the library, or schlepping their kids to school. How hot is that? Unlike most of the perfectly sculpted, empty-headed babes that took their place, these ten actresses could deliver the goods whether their clothes were on or off.

1 Annette Haven

She's one of porn's first divas—and she had the goods to back it up. Haven (who grew up Mormon) was a "ladies' lady"—refined, elegant, and in her case, overtly sexual. A string of jobs as a cabaret dancer and model led to some early movies with iconic porn director Alex De Renzy in the mid-'70s. Her striking features and considerable talents allowed Haven to pick and choose roles, partners—even positions (a rare privilege). A vocal feminist, she refused to appear in scenes that featured bondage or violence toward women, and never allowed her face to be defiled with the foul fluids of her male costars. She was cast at both ends of the spectrum—her petite frame being equally suited to the roles of "curious virgin" and "self-assured seductress."

A.K.A.: Annette Robinson

HIGHLIGHTS: *Barbara Broadcast* (1977), *V: The Hot One* (1978), *High School Memories* (1981)

CURRENTLY: Haven retired from porn in the late '80s. These days, she's married and raising a family in California.

it's everything you want

F

...AND LOTS OF IT!

starring
ANNETTE HAVEN
and JOHN LESLIE

with
SEKA
ANDERSON
CHRIS ANDERSON
BECKE BITTER
KANDI BARBOUR
MARY DARLING
GERALDINE GOLD
KASSY
RHONDA JO PETTY
LAURA SMITH
PIPER SMITH

produced by
DAVID I. FRAZER

directed by
SVETLANA

a CINETREX release
©1981

IN COLOR

WE DELIVER!!!

② Desiree Cousteau

She personifies the word "bubbly"—from her famously curvaceous body to her equally famous personality. The supposed Georgia native landed in Hollywood with mainstream dreams, and for a minute or two things looked promising. She scored a part in the cult favorite *Caged Heat* (1974), a movie that launched the career of future Oscar-winning director Jonathan Demme. But by the following year, she'd become Desiree Cousteau, porn actress. Her star-making role came in 1978, when Alex De Renzy cast her in *Pretty Peaches*—a movie that made the most of

Cousteau's ability to blend air-headed aloofness and raw sexuality. She wasn't the best actress of the classic bunch, but that wasn't important. Her boundless energy made her unique, and makes her movies required viewing. Cousteau's reasons for getting out of porn in the mid-'80s were just as mysterious as her reasons for getting in. Try as I might, I couldn't track her down.

A.K.A.: Deborah Clearbranch, Desiree Clearbranch

HIGHLIGHTS: *Pretty Peaches* (1978), *Hot and Saucy Pizza Girls* (1978), *Inside Desiree Cousteau* (1979)

CURRENTLY: Few know for sure. Depending on which rumor you believe, Cousteau is anything from a mental health professional in her home state of Georgia to a mental patient who was institutionalized after a nervous breakdown.

③ Kay Parker

Blessed with a pair of sizable natural assets, this free-spirited Englishwoman always carried herself like a serious actress (her porn debut was a fully clothed role in *V: The Hot One*). And while she was certainly better than most, it wasn't her acting that made her legendary. Maybe it was that reserved British demeanor, or the fact that she was a little older than many of her costars, but she always seemed out of place—*above* the industry. Like somebody's mom had accidentally wandered onto the set and wound up naked. And that, dear reader, is what made her unique—and hot. She spent most of her career playing undersexed moms and older/wiser/hornier mentors. Nowhere were these maternal qualities put to better use than in 1980's groundbreaking *Taboo*. After some fifty films, many of which remain in high demand, Parker left the business in 1986. One of the kindest souls you're likely to meet, Parker carries no regrets about her journey through the adult world.

A.K.A.: Jill Jackson, Kay Taylor

HIGHLIGHTS: *Sex World* (1978), *Taboo* (1980), *Sweet Young Foxes* (1983)

CURRENTLY: Parker keeps busy working as a spiritual counselor and healer in Los Angeles. You can see what she's up to at starsourceonline.com.

④ Ginger Lynn

She's the missing link—the bridge between the old business and the new. And though she was only active for one of porn's classic years, Ginger Lynn made such an impact that it would be a travesty to leave her off the list. This Illinois beauty came to California in the early '80s and found work as a *Penthouse* model. She made her film debut in 1984, and was almost instantly signed to an exclusive contract (as the first "Vivid Girl"—a title later held by Jenna Jameson). Ginger made headlines in the early '90s, first for her very public relationship with actor Charlie Sheen and later for her bust on tax-evasion charges. She ended up serving four and a half months in prison after violating her parole by testing positive for drugs. Ginger's since cleaned up her act, becoming a mother in 1996 and making a triumphant return to the business in 1999. Her comeback seemed over when she was diagnosed with cervical cancer the following year. But after undergoing treatment, she's cancer-free and back to work.

A.K.A.: Ginger Lynn Allen

HIGHLIGHTS: *On Golden Blonde* (1984), *The Pink Lagoon* (1984), *A Little Bit of Hanky Panky* (1984)

CURRENTLY: Ginger stays busy writing and performing in movies directed by fellow legend Veronica Hart.

⑤ Juliet Anderson

The epitome of the "mature" porn star. Anderson—a California native—had already lived a rich and varied life before stumbling into porn at the age of forty. She'd traveled the world teaching English to students in Japan and Greece, worked as a cocktail waitress in Miami, and produced radio shows in Finland. Following her 1978 debut in *Pretty Peaches* (opposite Desiree Cousteau [page 90]), Anderson appeared in several films before a string of hits made her a star in 1980. Roles in *Taboo*, *Talk Dirty to Me*, and *Aunt Peg* elevated Anderson to the top tier of porn-formers. Her turn as "Peg" was so popular that it spawned three sequels (to this day, many porn fans only

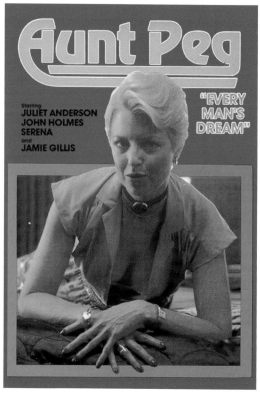

know her as "Aunt Peg"). In 1984, Anderson discovered another porn legend when she produced and directed a young Nina Hartley in *Educating Nina*. She left the business the same year after a dispute over the film's distribution.

A.K.A.: Aunt Peg, Judy Fallbrook

HIGHLIGHTS: *Aunt Peg* (1980), *Aunt Peg Goes Hollywood* (1981), *Educating Nina* (1984)

CURRENTLY: Still acting (she guest-starred on *The Sopranos*), Anderson also produced a video for older couples who want to improve their sex lives.

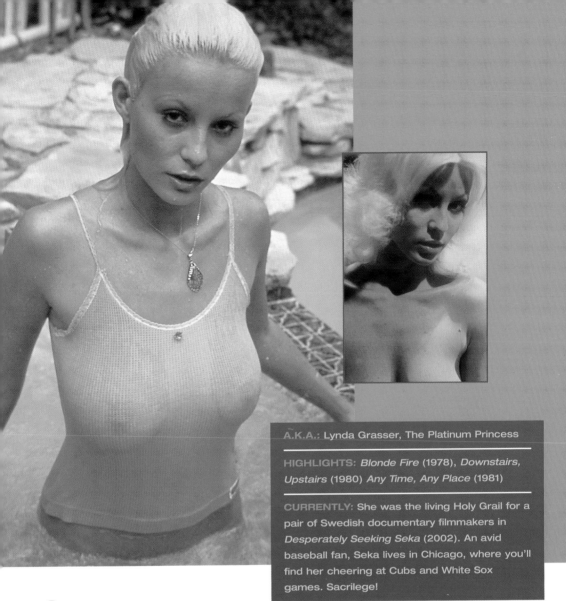

6 Seka

Seka (Croatian for "sister") is the personification of early '80s porn. The Virginia native had some early success in mainstream modeling, but the porno bug bit her while working in an adult bookstore. She moved to Los Angeles with the intent to make a name for herself in the adult world (unlike many of her fellow female legends, Seka didn't start out coveting a mainstream acting career). In 1978, she made her debut opposite John C. Holmes in the Johnny Wadd caper *Blonde Fire*. Her platinum exterior and sexual gusto quickly made her one of the most sought-after names in the business. But behind the scenes, two failed marriages and a stint in drug rehab threatened to derail her career before it even started. Seka pulled herself together, going on to star in more than one hundred films before her disappointing swan song, *American Garter* (1993).

⑦ Vanessa Del Rio

Del Rio was the first and greatest of all Latina porn stars—a Harlem-born Puerto Rican who had more curves than a bobsled track. The former Catholic schoolgirl oozed sex from every pore. One of the most uninhibited classic performers, Del Rio was once anally fisted by a dwarf—Louie Short Stud, the little Nazi from *Kate and the Indians*. Her voluptuous body and sexual openness got Vanessa in the door, but it was her legendary "oral presentations" that made her a sensation in the late '70s and early '80s. Some say she was born without a gag reflex, others think she just took pleasure in her work. Because of her proclivity for loud, passionate lovemaking, she was usually cast as an insatiable sex fiend. After close to one hundred movies, Del Rio retired from the scene in 1986 and settled down in New York.

A.K.A.: Ursula Passarell

HIGHLIGHTS: *Tigresses . . . and Other Man-Eaters* (1979), *The Filthy Rich* (1980), *Dracula Exotica* (1981)

CURRENTLY: Voluptuous and sultry as ever, Del Rio continues to strut her stuff online. Her Web site offers members everything from current nude photos to private one-on-one phone calls.

⑧ Marilyn Chambers

Her childhood was right out of the WASP handbook. Born and raised in Westport, Connecticut (your hopelessly white author's childhood digs), Chambers's fresh-faced teen beauty earned her work as a print model in New York. Her wholesome face was even chosen to grace the cover of Ivory Snow boxes nationwide. Does it get any more "all-American"? Soon it was on to California and a role in the 1970 Barbra Streisand film *The Owl and the Pussycat*. But after a promising start, the roles dried up, and Chambers found herself looking for a new opportunity in San

Francisco. It came when she was spotted by producers Jim and Artie Mitchell. They were so passionate about having Marilyn star in *Behind the Green Door* (1972) that they gave up an unheard-of 10 percent of the profits. Her youth and innocence helped *Green Door* become a huge hit, but as Marilyn's career matured, so did her sexual prowess. By 1980, the once-demure Ivory Snow girl had become *Insatiable*.

A.K.A.: Marilyn Briggs, Evelyn Lang, Marilyn Taylor

HIGHLIGHTS: *Behind the Green Door* (1972), *Resurrection of Eve* (1973), *Insatiable* (1980)

CURRENTLY: Like Ginger Lynn, Chambers has returned to porn after a long hiatus. In 1999 she starred in *Still Insatiable*, a sequel to the 1980 classic. It was directed by fellow porn legend Veronica Hart (see page 99).

⑨ Georgina Spelvin

In 1972, frustrated Broadway hoofer Dorothy May was having trouble paying her bills. She'd come a long way—overcoming polio as a child and making her way out of the Texas suburbs. She'd even flirted with mainstream success—serving as Shirley MacLaine's dance double in *Sweet Charity* (1969). But times were tough, and when friend Harry Reems approached her about a catering job on a low-budget skin flick, she couldn't say no. The movie was *The Devil in Miss Jones* (1973)—and production had barely begun when its female star chickened out. Quicker than you can say "breakfast burrito," Dorothy was asked if she wanted a (debatable) promotion to leading lady. Still clinging to hopes of a mainstream career, she feminized "George Spelvin"—the name actors traditionally use when they'd rather remain anonymous. The film was a sensation, and over the next decade Spelvin became one of the busiest and most revered actresses in the business.

A.K.A.: Dorothy May, Ruth Raymond

HIGHLIGHTS: *The Devil in Miss Jones* (1973), *3 a.m.* (1976), *The Ecstasy Girls* (1979)

CURRENTLY: Spelvin lives in Los Angeles, where she works in graphic design and makes the occasional mainstream cameo.

10 Veronica Hart

Born and raised in Las Vegas, Jane Hamilton was probably the world's least-likely porn star. She was a serious actress—trained in theater at the University of Nevada, Las Vegas. She'd performed at the Kennedy Center and modeled in Europe. But after trying her hand at everything from managing a rock band to answering phones at *Psychology Today*, Hamilton hadn't been able to nail down a steady paycheck. That is, until a friend introduced her to some people in "the business." She was reborn "Veronica Hart" in *Women in Love* (1979), launching a brief but extraordinary career as one of porn's best actresses and most enthusiastic lovers. However, her stint as a hardcore performer lasted only four years. In 1984, with a new husband and baby, she couldn't bring herself to have sex on camera anymore. But her relationship with adult film wasn't over. Hart returned to porn as a director in the mid-'90s, and she's been responsible for some of the best features in recent memory.

A.K.A.: Jane Hamilton, Kathryn Stanleigh, Randee Styles

HIGHLIGHTS: *A Scent of Heather* (1981), *Wanda Whips Wall Street* (1981), *The Playgirl* (1982)

CURRENTLY: Besides being one of the industry's most respected producer/directors, Hart continues to act (fully clothed) in shows like *Six Feet Under* and movies like *Magnolia* and *Timeline*.

☆ the gentlemen

They're called "Woodsmen." "Cocksmiths." The men who have the heavy equipment and know how to operate it under pressure. And unlike their female counterparts, there's no faking it. When the lights are shining, the camera's rolling, and the crew's drooling, they have to stand tall. Yes, it's harder than it looks (assuming all goes well). But the men on this list brought more than inches and reliability to the table. They brought charisma, talent, and (I know, I know) longevity to a business that's removed more studs than a general contractor. Here are ten "pillars" of the adult community.

1 Ron Jeremy

In the 1970s, New York City's porn industry was exploding—and Ron Jeremy Hyatt (no relation to the hotel chain) had nothing to do with it. No, Ron was a special-education teacher. But his teaching career suffered a deathblow in 1978, when Ron's girlfriend sent his picture to *Playgirl*. Soon Jeremy was packing them in for live stage shows (one of his specialties was giving himself fellatio). His film debut came in 1979, and he's been in demand ever since. Quite an achievement for a guy nicknamed "The Hedgehog" due to his abundantly hairy body. But it's that average appearance that's proven the key to his staying power. Well, okay—his gigantic penis hasn't hurt. In the '90s, Jeremy transitioned from porn star to pop culture icon; his mustachioed mug showed up on T-shirts and TV sets, and he was a frequent guest on *The Jerry Springer Show* and other "legitimate" outlets. He continues to work in adult films on both sides of the camera, and he's become a master of the "gimmick" porno. We have Ron to thank for signing John Wayne Bobbitt and Divine Brown to porno deals. You'll also find him performing stand-up, lecturing across the country, and serving as technical advisor on films like *Boogie Nights* (1997) and *Nine 1/2 Weeks* (1986).

A.K.A.: Ron Hyatt, David Elliot, Bill Blackman, Nicholas Pera, Hedgehog

HIGHLIGHTS: *The Blonde Next Door* (1982), *Snatchbuckler* (1985), *The Maddams Family* (1993)

CURRENTLY: After cameos in mainstream movies like *Detroit Rock City* (1999) and *Reindeer Games* (2000), Jeremy landed a spot on the WB's *The Surreal Life*. He continues to turn up on talk shows, T-shirts, and at conventions from coast to coast.

A.K.A.: John Curtis Estes, Johnny Wadd, Long John Wadd)

——————————————

HIGHLIGHTS: *Tell Them Johnny Wadd Is Here* (1975), *The Senator's Daughter* (1979), *Prisoner of Paradise* (1980)

② John C. Holmes

Speak softly and carry a big stick. Holmes spoke much more softly than his piercing features suggest, and he carried the biggest stick of them all. Hollywood has based movies (*Wonderland*, *Boogie Nights*) on different aspects of his life and career— mostly his troubled final years and monstrous member. The *real* Holmes began his journey as a sensitive Ohio boy at odds with his stepfather. With mom's permission, John joined the army before his eighteenth birthday and spent three years stationed in Germany. When his stint was up, he headed to California, and it wasn't long before smut peddlers sniffed out the gold mine between his legs. Starting with loops and low-budget skin flicks, Holmes carved a name for himself as a reliable woodsman. But as the films got bigger and his fame spread, his self-destructive tendencies emerged. John's marriage crumbled and he fell in love with an underage girl (he'd later pimp her for money while running from the law). He also fell in love with cocaine, and spent every porn penny he earned buying more. When that was gone, he turned to burglary. The bottom came when he was accused of being an accomplice in the Wonderland Avenue murders—the beating deaths of two men and two women. He was eventually acquitted and made an attempt to salvage his porn career. But any hope of a comeback was dashed when Holmes was diagnosed with AIDS. He died in 1988, leaving behind a legacy of hundreds of films.

③ John Leslie

When John Leslie Nuzo arrived in New York City in the early '60s, he was just like any other Midwestern boy with big dreams. A skilled painter, illustrator, and musician, he tried his hand at a number of artistic jobs—but none of them covered the rent. It wasn't until the swinging '70s that John finally found his true calling. By now the Midwestern boy had matured into a smooth operator—a good-looking, sharply dressed, and silver-tongued embodiment of the disco-era stud. He started making movies (sans "Nuzo") at age thirty, and his sophistication and hyperconfident demeanor quickly made him a hot commodity. Off camera, he was anything but a porn cliché—a lover of art and fine wine who was noted for his kindness to female costars. Appropriately, Leslie was (by far) the most popular porn star of his day with female movie-goers. Though he wasn't formally trained, his acting skills are considered by some to be the best ever seen in adult filmdom. In the mid-'80s, Leslie was one of the first performers to move behind the camera, going on to direct "too-good-for-porn" efforts like *Dog Walker* (1994) and *Curse of the Catwoman* (1992).

A.K.A.: John Leslie Dupree, John Lestor, Lenny Kent

HIGHLIGHTS: *Sex World* (1978), *Aunt Peg's Fulfillment* (1981), *Nothing to Hide* (1981)

CURRENTLY: Leslie remains busy directing (and occasionally appearing in) pornos for Evil Angel Productions and his own John Leslie Productions.

You've heard all the different formulas: Your pet's name plus the street you grew up on; your middle name plus your mother's maiden name. Problem is, you run the risk of winding up with "Cookie Route 6" or "Eugene Papadopolous." Fine names indeed, but not befitting a porn star.

What's in a Porn Name?

The truth? There's no one equation. Crafting your *nom de porn* is an art, not a science—the process is different for everyone. That said, allow me to offer a few suggestions:

Originality: Avoid done-to-death porn staples like "Sky," "Rain," and "Wood." Rule of thumb: If it's something that occurs in nature, it's a bad porn name.

Play on Words: "Jenna Jameson" aside, the best way to make your name stick is to parody something (or someone) famous. "Max Headroom" becomes "Max Hardcore"; "Jewel of the Nile" becomes "Jewel DeNyle," and so on.

Illustrative: What comes to mind when you hear it? It's no coincidence that men often use variations of "Steel" or "Rock" while women prefer "Cherry" and "Candy." Mmmm, Candy.

Now that you know the guidelines, let's take a look at these real porn names and see how they measure up. (And for additional inspiration, check out Nathan Garfinkel's *Fluffy Cumsalot, Porn Star* (2003)—a documentary about the real stories behind many of the biggest names in porn.)

allysin chains

Violet Blue: First of all, make up your mind. Second, your name is so uninspired that I've already forgotten it.

Allysin Chains: A trifecta. Parodies a famous rock band, incorporates the word "sin," and conjures images of bondage. An original and memorable porn name.

Chris Charming: What? Who cares if you're "charming"? You're a meat puppet, buddy—here to do one thing and one thing only. Leave the charm to Lorenzo Lamas.

Jaden: First of all, "Jade" is one of the most overused names in porndom. There's "Kendra Jade," "Jewels Jade," "Jade Marcela," "Golden Jade," "Layla Jade," "Sabrina Jade" and, well . . . "Jade." Second, what the hell is a "Jaden?" Unoriginal and unmemorable.

Lynden Johnson: If you're a porn actress who simply *has* to name herself after a president, don't pick Lyndon Johnson. He was, perhaps, our least sexy commander in chief (right up there with Rutherford B. Hayes). Almost *any* president would've been better: Georgette W. Bushless, Grover Cleavage, Millie Fillmore, Chesty Arthur . . .

Anna Malle: Stupid? Yes, but evocative and easy to remember, too. Anna claims that the spelling of her *nom de porn* was taken from French film director Louis Malle—the man who brought us *My Dinner with Andre* (1981). Because nothing says "hot" like two guys sitting at a table and talking for two hours.

Nadia Nyce: A winner on so many levels. It's alliterative, suggestive, and to my knowledge, the only porn name that poses a question ("Naughty or nice?").

Wesley Pipes: I can't think of a better porn moniker for a well-hung black man. Wait, yes I can: Cuba Wooding Jr. Hmm . . . no, I can't.

4 Jamie Gillis

When it comes to raw acting talent, nobody can touch Gillis. He's the Pacino of porn. The Brando of blue movies. Born in New York City, he trained as a serious actor at Columbia University and appeared in off-Broadway shows in the early '70s. While making his living as a cab driver, Gillis answered an ad for nude modeling, and a porn career was born. Early on, his acting skills made him the "go-to guy" when the script called for a rapist or psychopath. After all, the dirty DeNiro could do "crazy" better than anyone. But he was equally convincing as the refined cosmopolitan (*The Opening of Misty Beethoven*) or the horror icon (*Dracula Sucks*). Sexually speaking, nothing was off limits to the openly bisexual Gillis. His flair for bondage and rough style of lovemaking are legend. Like all of porn's aging males, he stepped into the director's chair in the '80s. One of his more successful efforts, *On the Prowl* (1989), was famously parodied in *Boogie Nights*. Gillis roamed the

streets of San Francisco in a limousine looking for average guys to climb in and make it with a porn-fessional actress. The movie is one of the earliest forays into pro-am (see page 138) and gonzo filmmaking.

A.K.A.: James Rugman, Buster Hymen, Ronny Morgan

HIGHLIGHTS: *The Opening of Misty Beethoven* (1976), *Coming of Angels* (1977), *Vista Valley P.T.A.* (1981)

CURRENTLY: The reclusive Gillis makes his home in San Francisco, but remains active in adult films. Recently, he's had roles in upscale productions like *Sunset Stripped* and *Edge Play* (along with fellow classic legend Marilyn Chambers).

⑤ Richard Pacheco

Before getting his rocks off in the movies, Pacheco the construction worker was breaking them for five bucks a day. The married college graduate had considered becoming everything from a journalist to a rabbi (that's no joke—he actually applied to a seminary) when he was offered a role in *Candy Stripers* (1978). With approval from the coolest wife who ever lived, Pacheco embarked on a decade-long adventure that would take him soaring to the heights of smut. His gentle features usually landed him roles as the "lucky geek"—the glasses-wearing goof who's seduced by the predatory female. He was a surprisingly good actor, turning in convincing (and occasionally moving) performances in many of his movies. But everything changed when AIDS appeared. He had a wife and babies, and wasn't willing to put them at risk. When Pacheco began insisting on condoms in 1985, his career imploded overnight. He stuck around for a few years behind the camera, working as an assistant director for his friend John Leslie. But watching people have sex all day without joining in proved too torturous, and he soon left the business for good.

A.K.A.: Dewey Alexander, Mack Howard

HIGHLIGHTS: *Talk Dirty to Me* (1980), *The Dancers* (1981), *Summer of '72* (1982)

CURRENTLY: Pacheco's performing days are behind him, though he still makes infrequent appearances at industry trade shows and plans to publish a book about his adventures in porn. And yes, he's still married to the coolest wife who ever lived.

6 Paul Thomas

Born to a wealthy Illinois family, young Philip Toubus was barely in his twenties when Hollywood came calling. After starring in the Broadway production of *Hair* (1968), he made his big screen debut as Peter in the film version of *Jesus Christ Superstar* (1973). Toubus was promptly snatched up by the William Morris Agency and landed guest spots on a couple of TV dramas—but he soon tired of the constant rejection of the audition process. As fate would have it, he met famed porn directors Jim and Artie Mitchell on a trip to San Francisco in 1974. It took some convincing, but soon Toubus (rechristened "Paul Thomas") was starring in sex loops for the Mitchell brothers. Eager to be a leading man, he made his porn feature debut in *The Autobiography of a Flea* (1976), and his dreams of stardom came true—though not exactly as he'd planned. He shared the screen with virtually every important porn star over the next two decades, and appeared in countless classics. But unlike many of his contemporaries (who never tasted mainstream success), he's admitted to having regrets about getting into the adult business. Almost thirty years and hundreds of films after his encounter with the Mitchell brothers, Thomas remains one of the biggest players in the game.

A.K.A.: Phil Tobias, Grady Sutton, Judy Blue

HIGHLIGHTS: *Candy Stripers* (1978), *Lipps & McCain* (1978), *Dracula Sucks* (1979)

CURRENTLY: Thomas has become one of the adult world's busiest directors, helming a string of porn's bigger-budget features for Vivid Video.

7 Herschel Savage

He's a journeyman porn star—a performer whose persistence and reliability have given him a career spanning four decades. Savage's critics will remind you of all the things he's not: a particularly gifted actor. An innovative director. Fine, but it's what he is that counts: a mix of sexually blessed macho man and down-to-earth fishing buddy. A nice Jewish boy with a reputation for being friendly and hardworking. Like many of his fellow legends, Savage's porno journey began in the New York City of the 1970s. He was just another strug-

gling actor when a friend (porn actor Richard Bolla) introduced him to the adult world. Savage ended up making hundreds of films before his retirement in the late '80s. After his marriage fell apart in 1995, Savage found himself looking for a new challenge. A friend urged him to come out of retirement, and in 1997, he set out to conquer the industry for a second time. Savage remarried in 2001, this time to a striking young adult actress named Wanda Curtis.

A.K.A.: Vic Falcone, Nick Barris, Cornell Hayes

HIGHLIGHTS: *The Satisfiers of Alpha Blue* (1981), *8 to 4* (1981), *Up 'n Coming* (1983)

CURRENTLY: With more than 1,100 films under his belt, Savage remains a popular performer and director.

⑧ Harry Reems

The man had more hair above his neck than a primate. Those eyebrows. That mustache. He was like a living, breathing Ned Flanders. He was also the first man to become a certified American porn star. Like many of the classic studs who would follow in his footsteps, Reems (Herb Streicher) had his roots in the New York theater. But the former Marine needed cash, so he started making underground loops in the early '70s. In one series, he played an eccentric doctor opposite a newcomer named Linda Lovelace. Sensing potential, director Gerard Damiano shot some connecting footage in 1972, and *Deep Throat* was born. (If you watch the film, you'll notice Reems's hair change length from scene to scene). The following year, *The Devil in Miss Jones* solidified Reems as the stud to beat. He gave interviews to the mainstream media, lectured on college campuses, and earned a small fortune headlining dozens of features during the next decade. But his meteoric career fizzled when drugs and alcohol got the best of him. Soon Reems, who'd once earned thousands of dollars a week, was broke—sleeping on the street and rummaging through Dumpsters to support his habit. But wait—there's a happy ending! After a stint in rehab, he cleaned up his act and left the business for good. In the '90s, Reems got hitched and found Jesus (just like Ned Flanders).

A.K.A.: Herbert Streicher, Herb Stryker, Bruce Gilchrist, Bob Walters

HIGHLIGHTS: *Deep Throat* (1972), *Sex Wish* (1976), *Meatball* (1978)

CURRENTLY: Reems owns a successful real estate company in Utah (he continues to use the name "Harry Reems" in business dealings). He and his wife are active members of their community and Methodist church.

❾ Tom Byron

He's the Ricky Schroder of porn. America's watched little Tommy Byron grow from the lanky high school virgin into the pierced and tattooed star of *Operation Just Cooze* (2001). On second thought, maybe he's nothing like Ricky Schroder. This Texas native entered porn in 1982 after working at an adult novelty store. Though he was twenty-one at the time, his unusually boyish face and unusually giant tool made him perfect for movies like *Kinky Business* (1985) and *Up 'n Coming* (1983). He was the "dirty little boy"—fantasizing about what it's like to have sex, then finding out. The best of these early movies is *Private Teacher* (1983), in which he's lovingly tutored by Kay Parker and Honey Wilder. As the business changed in the 1980s, so did Byron—from innocent kid to long-haired rocker, from sensitive student to aggressive stud. He briefly dated Traci Lords, shed his bony frame, and started directing his own movies in the mid-'90s. Byron's newer films (*Meat Pushin' in the Seat Cushion* [2003]) aren't likely to earn him widespread critical acclaim, but they are likely to earn him a fortune.

A.K.A.: Thomas Bryan Taliaferro Jr.

HIGHLIGHTS: *Private Teacher* (1983), *Tomboy* (1983), *The Woman in Pink* (1984)

CURRENTLY: With over two thousand films to his credit, Byron announced his retirement from performing in 2002. The following year, he created Evolution Erotica, a production company dedicated to "the darker side of sexuality."

10 Joey Silvera

By all accounts, Joey Silvera is extremely likable and extremely laid back. The kind of guy who punctuates every sentence with "man" or "you know?" Yet this ex-hippie façade does injustice to the originality and intensity that he's been bringing to porno for thirty years. Silvera started making loops in 1973 and features shortly thereafter. Director Alex De Renzy cast him in several early films that helped solidify his reputation as a talented actor/stud: *Femmes de Sade* (1976), *Baby Face* (1977), and *Pretty Peaches* (1978). His early roles were often tough guys, pimps, or criminals. Maybe it was those laser beam eyes. More likely, it was the mustache.

But eventually, producers discovered Silvera's quick wit (and bizarre imagination—more evident in his directing). Being around for thirty years has its perks—just ask Silvera, who's been with everyone from Seka to Ginger Lynn to Jenna Jameson. And since all aging porn studs become porn directors (it's practically the law in California), Silvera moved behind the camera in 1995.

A.K.A.: Joey Civera, Neil Long, Tony Nacivers

HIGHLIGHTS: *Baby Face* (1977), *Sex World* (1978), *The Dancers* (1981)

CURRENTLY: Still performing after four decades, Silvera also directs movies for Evil Angel—notably the depraved *Butt Row* series. My personal favorites include *Fame Is a Whore on Butt Row* (1996) and *White Men Can't Iron on Butt Row* (1997).

He's perhaps the only man to take a bullet for porn (literally—he was shot on March 6, 1978, by white supremacist Joseph Paul Franklin, who'd been enraged by an interracial photo spread in Flynt's *Hustler* magazine). Despite that, he's spent the better part of his life standing up (figuratively—the shooting left him in a wheelchair) to government censorship and conservative anti-porn efforts, even though Flynt himself once flirted with becoming an evangelical Christian. Some of Larry's greatest hits (and misses):

Larry Flynt: Great American Porn Hero

* **1983:** The same year he announces his intention to run for president against Ronald Reagan, Flynt shows up to court wearing an American flag as a diaper. Note to self: On second thought, don't hire Larry Flynt to run my presidential campaign.

* **1998:** During President Clinton's impeachment proceedings, he offers $1 million for proof of sexual misconduct by Republican lawmakers. The stunt leads to the resignation of House Speaker-elect Bob Livingston after evidence of his numerous infidelities is uncovered.

* **2003:** Flynt runs for governor of California in the recall election of Governor Gray Davis. Flynt's slogan? "A Smut Peddler Who Cares." He receives 17,458 votes.

Classic Crossovers

Before *The Godfather* (1972) and *Apocalypse Now* (1979), Francis Ford Coppola produced the "nudie cutie" *Tonight for Sure* (1962). (Designed to push the limits of 1960s decency laws, nudie cuties were loosely plotted, poorly acted, bare-breasted, penetration-free precursors to the pornos we know and love today.) And while porn isn't exactly a rocket to fame and fortune, Coppola's not the first person to bounce off the skin-flick springboard.

Brian Heidik

Who? All right, so maybe porn didn't bring him fame, but it definitely put him on the path to fortune. Heidik starred in a number of soft-core flicks before deciding to audition for *Survivor: Thailand*. Halfway through production, CBS was embroiled in a mini-scandal when his adult-film past was uncovered by The Smoking Gun. But the network stood by its man, and Heidik went on to win the million bucks.

Jenna Jameson

She's the mother of all crossover stars. And unlike 99.99 percent of the young women who get into the adult business, Jenna has reaped huge rewards from porn. She's appeared in network dramas (*Nash Bridges*) and mainstream movies (*Private Parts*), and she's lent her voice to prime-time cartoons (*Family Guy*) and top-selling video games (*Grand Theft Auto: Vice City*). She remains the biggest

star in porn, while serving as the CEO of her own management, production, and licensing company, ClubJenna, Inc. In 2004, she published her autobiography, *How to Make Love Like a Porn Star: A Cautionary Tale*. Just like everything else she touches, it became an instant best seller.

Ron Jeremy

It's a journey that's taken him from *Spermbusters to The Surreal Life*. Jeremy's defied all the odds one can defy: becoming a porn stud despite his looks; becoming a household name despite being a porn stud. He's built an industry around himself—licensing that unmistakable mug to T-shirt companies, giving lectures at colleges around the country, and getting himself a spot on a prime-time reality series owned by Warner Bros.

Traci Lords

After almost single-handedly destroying the porn industry in 1986 (see page 28), Lords has managed to string together a decent mainstream acting career. Her big break came when John Waters cast her opposite Johnny Depp in *Cry-Baby* (1990). Since then, Traci's shared the screen with Wesley Snipes in *Blade* (1998) and landed a recurring role on NBC's *Profiler*.

Sylvester Stallone

Sly indeed. Stallone was a struggling twenty-three-year-old actor when he starred in *The Party at Kitty and Stud's* (1970), a terribly made hard-core feature that was later softened up and re-released as *Italian Stallion* (1976). As for that question burning a hole in your mind? The answer is "yes." You see it. A lot. Stallone received $200 for his work in *Kitty*, and to his credit, never made any attempts to suppress the movie after he became a superstar.

Joan Crawford (?)

Rumors persist that a young Crawford (born Lucille LeSueur) made several "loops"—or pornographic shorts—while working in a Chicago brothel. While there's no way of knowing for sure, she certainly had a classic porn star childhood: Her parents separated before she was born, and by age sixteen, she'd known three fathers. Crawford never claimed she was a good girl. She once remarked, "If you want to see the girl next door, go next door."

☆ the ladies in waiting

Unless you live in cave (or a convent), you probably know the name Jenna Jameson. After all, she's a once-in-a-generation porn star—a woman whose fame can't be confined to the genre. But she isn't the *only* superstar in adult films. There are a handful of women—"ladies in waiting"—who are poised to take over as reigning porn goddess should Jenna's star ever fade. And like their queen, each offers more than your average smutstress. A few likely candidates:

① Tera Patrick

Thomas Jefferson wrote that "all men are created equal." When I look at these pictures, I feel like building a time machine, going back to 1776, and punching him in the face. Tera Patrick is better than "equal." She's outstanding. And get this—she's smart, too. How many porn stars do you know who have a degree in microbiology and speak fluent Hungarian? The answer is "one." Patrick recently married Biohazard front man/lucky-son-of-a-bitch Evan Seinfeld. Her current contract with Vivid Video stipulates that he's the only stud she'll work with. Great. Just great.

A.K.A.: Linda Shapiro, Sadie Jordan, Brooke Thomas

HIGHLIGHTS: *Sex Island* (1999), *Forbidden Tales* (2001), *Island Fever* (2001)

② Devon

This 5'2" bombshell has the "cute" market cornered, and so far, her porn career has been something of a fairytale: Devon was just a simple cabaret dancer in Pennsylvania when a boyfriend encouraged her to try porn in 1998. A year later, she was one its biggest stars. Unlike most of her contemporaries, she's never had to slum it in ultracheap gonzo or fetish videos. In fact, most of her starring roles have come in big-budget action/porn or fantasy/porn movies. (Just don't confuse her with *Devon Davis*, the ex-porn star who's now married to Korn front man, Jonathan Davis.)

A.K.A.: Devin Striker

HIGHLIGHTS: *Blown Away* (1999), *Rush* (2002), *No Limits* (2003)

3 Jessie Jane

By 2004, Jessie Jane was a one-woman industry. Her films were all big-budget best sellers. She had her own line of sex toys and a popular Web site. She traveled the country making appearances and doing press. "So what?" you ask? Her career *began* in 2003. Not since Ginger Lynn has a porn starlet gotten so big so quickly. This former tomboy was born in the 1980s and found some success as a bikini model. But she wanted stardom, and knew she'd find it in adult features. Drawn to her enthusiasm and Veronica Lake-ish beauty, Digital Playground signed her to a contract on the spot.

A.K.A.: Jesse Jane

HIGHLIGHTS: *Beat the Devil* (2003), *Erotique* (2003), *Loaded* (2004)

☆ the directors

They didn't make "sex movies"—they made movies that happened to feature sex. The classic era's best directors were part of the wave of young talent that swept the film industry in the early '70s—the same wave that carried Steven Spielberg, George Lucas, and Martin Scorsese. And while they never reached that level of skill or success, they aspired to it. That alone makes them worth remembering.

① Anthony Spinelli

He was probably the greatest porn director who ever lived. The skill and sensitivity in Spinelli's movies was a holdover from his days in mainstream filmmaking. He produced and acted in *One Potato, Two Potato* (1964), an Oscar-nominated, racially charged movie that won acclaim at the Cannes Film Festival. But a string of bad luck and severed relationships left him on the outs, and Weston turned to porn to pay the rent. While his Hollywood dreams faded away, his talent remained intact. Spinelli managed to elicit beauty and emotion from screw flicks. That's the creative equivalent of painting a Rembrandt with dog crap. It's remarkable. He had no time, no money, and nobody kissing his ass—but he always pulled it off. Spinelli stopped making films in the mid-'90s and died in 2000. Had he stayed in the mainstream, you have to wonder how far he could've gone.

> **A.K.A.:** Sam Weinstein, Sam Weston, Wes Brown
>
> ---
>
> **HIGHLIGHTS:** *Sex World* (1978), *High School Memories* (1978), *The Dancers* (1978)

② Russ Meyer

I can almost hear the purists going crazy. "Russ Meyer never directed a porno!" Technically, they're right—while his films were overflowing with naked women, they were sadly devoid of penetration. Still, he did more to legitimize "trashy" movies than almost any human being in the twentieth century. His success in the late '50s and '60s made it possible for films like *Deep Throat* to find distribution in

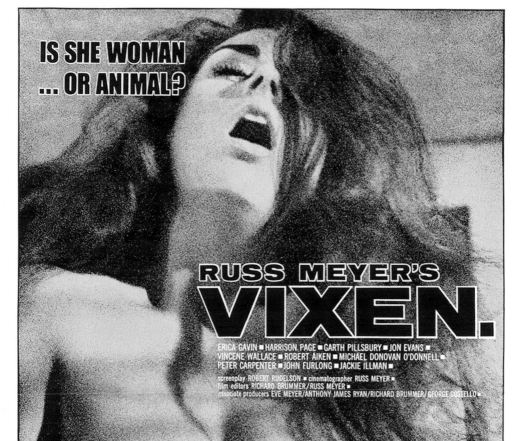

IS SHE WOMAN ... OR ANIMAL?

RUSS MEYER'S
VIXEN.

ERICA GAVIN ■ HARRISON. PAGE ■ GARTH PILLSBURY ■ JON EVANS ■
VINCENE WALLACE ■ ROBERT AIKEN ■ MICHAEL DONOVAN O'DONNELL ■
PETER CARPENTER ■ JOHN FURLONG ■ JACKIE ILLMAN ■
screenplay ROBERT RUDELSON ■ cinematographer RUSS MEYER ■
film editors RICHARD BRUMMER/RUSS MEYER ■
associate producers EVE MEYER/ANTHONY JAMES RYAN/RICHARD BRUMMER/GEORGE COSTELLO ■

IN EASTMANCOLOR ■ RESTRICTED TO ADULT AUDIENCES ■ AN EVE PRODUCTION

ONLY TODAY'S DEMENTED SOCIETY COULD MAKE SUCH AN ANIMAL A WOMAN ... OR SUCH A WOMAN AN ANIMAL.

the '70s. Even more important, hits like *Vixen!* (1968) and *Beyond the Valley of the Dolls* (1970) showed Hollywood that there was serious money to be made in the exploitation genre, opening the door for a whole new generation of boundary-busting filmmakers. Sadly, Meyer passed away on September 18, 2004.

A.K.A.: King Leer

HIGHLIGHTS: *The Immoral Mr. Teas* (1959), *Faster, Pussycat! Kill! Kill!* (1965), *Beyond the Valley of the Dolls* (1970)

3 Gerard Damiano

Damiano seems to be two people—the goofy ex-hairdresser who made *Deep Throat* and *Let My Puppets Come*, and the guilt-ridden Catholic who made *The Devil in Miss Jones* and *The Satisfiers of Alpha Blue*. The first guy's important—after all, he made the biggest porno of all time. But it's the second guy I'm interested in. With *DMJ*, Damiano followed up the cultural phenomenon of *Throat* with something of a cinematic apology—a film that says, "If you're a slut, you'll wind up in hell." That same original sin is evident in *Satisfiers*, a film that says, "Having sex just for the sake of having sex is wrong." Damiano's movies rarely had the high-gloss production values of his competitors', but he was always trying to do something that seemed outrageous to everyone else. You've gotta love the guy for that.

A.K.A.: D. Furred, Jerry Gerard, Al Gork

HIGHLIGHTS: *The Devil in Miss Jones* (1973), *Fantasy* (1979), *The Satisfiers of Alpha Blue* (1981)

With very few exceptions, most of today's porn "directors"—yes, I threw down the quotes—are really little more than guys holding video cameras. At best, they're guys watching monitors and barking orders like "closer" and "much closer." But hope springs eternal in a few individuals who continue to make *movies.* You know—those things with stories, dialogue, and acting? These brave souls have resisted the temptations of gonzo to carry the torch of the classics.

4 James Avalon

A man who feels just as comfortable discussing Fellini as fellatio. Avalon's films are dark and edgy, dealing with themes like death and bondage in his unique visual style. On set, his brow is constantly furrowed. He wants to get it right. He wants it to look amazing. You'll even catch him sitting with an actress to discuss the emotional content of a scene (a revelation that could ruin his porn career). Avalon's one of the few adult filmmakers who can use the words "vision" and "metaphor" without being laughed out of the room. After twenty years in the business, he's seen every porn cliché in the book, and he's determined to avoid them. His stylistic shooting and often dream-like settings have earned him a reputation as porn's "artiest" director.

A.K.A.: Mondo Tundra

HIGHLIGHTS: *Red Vibe Diaries* (1997), *Les Vampyres* (2000), *Taboo 2001* (2001)

⑤ Nic Andrews

Andrews brings the Michael Bay/Jerry Bruckheimer mentality to porn: Guns are sexy; girls are sexy. Girls with guns? Orgasmic. His movies are full-blown (pardon the expression) productions in a business dominated by micro-budgeted bangers.

Andrews's work pushes the envelope of what's possible in the full-penetration world—car chases, huge explosions, and stunts are just a few of his staples. He's always looking for a way to incorporate Hollywood-level effects—always trying to make bigger, shinier films. His ambitious style has earned the young director's movies nine AVN awards and counting. Makes you wonder what he could do with a $100 million budget.

HIGHLIGHTS: *Rush* (2002), *No Limits* (2003), *Loaded* (2004)

4

what to watch, where to find it

For the newcomer, entering the sprawling world of smut can be intimidating—even embarrassing. I suspect millions go their entire adult lives without setting foot in the curtained-off section of the local video store—not for lack of interest, but for lack of courage. They live a tragically porn-less existence, afraid of being spotted by someone they know or, worse, afraid they'll really, really like what lies beyond that curtain. This chapter will help you conquer those fears and lead you confidently down the path to porn happiness.

Whether you've just turned eighteen or eighty, rushing headlong into adult films without the proper training is just plain irresponsible. Watching a porno without knowing its contents is like playing Russian roulette with your sanity. You'd better be sure, because all it takes is one unexpected image to crush your libido like an eggshell. Sure, categories like "Anal" and "Interracial" are self-explanatory. But what about "Bukkake" or "Pony Play"? In the interest of avoiding surprises, here's an introduction to some of the popular genres at your disposal. Just remember, folks: safety first.

Amateur

Everybody's a pornographer these days. And there's nothing wrong with rolling a little tape in the bedroom now and again, so long as you accept the inevitability of it winding up on the Internet. What sets "amateurs" apart is that they *intentionally* make their tapes available to the public—tapes featuring flabby midsections, razor-burned groins, and time/date stamps at the bottom of the screen. For a meager sum, average Joes and Janes license their home movies to big companies, which package them with other amateurs and reap big profits. If you're into hotness, I suggest you seek gratification elsewhere. But if you crave out-of-focus butt pimples, then let me be the first to congratulate you.

TURN-ONS: There's a certain voyeuristic adrenaline rush one gets when watching "real" people have sex.

TURN-OFFS: There's a reason these people aren't porn stars.

SAMPLE TITLE: *Are You XXXperienced* (2001)

ATM

Like me, you probably hoped this was some weird facet of porn where people got off by taking money out of their checking accounts. If only it were so. Unfortunately, in the adult world ATM means "Ass to Mouth." I invite your imagination to run wild for a moment. Now, there's no actual *excreting* going on (we'll get to that later), but there *is* the hygienically challenged act of . . . how can I put this . . . playing musical orifices without pausing to use a moist towelette? What's really astounding about this genre is its popularity. Virtually every adult retailer carries some of the hundreds of ATM titles on the market.

> **TURN-ONS:** Who doesn't savor the flavor of fresh ass?
>
> **TURN-OFFS:** It's . . . what's the word I'm looking for? Ah, yes. "Disgusting."
>
> **SAMPLE TITLE:** *Grand Theft Anal* (2003)

BDSM

True believers will scoff at the fact that I'm combining bondage and domination along with sadomasochism. Technically, they're three separate schools of thought. However, all three virtually guarantee the following: leather-clad femmes stomping on testicles with high heels; whips, chains, and candle wax; masked men eagerly begging to be spanked; and, of course, nipple clamps. BDSM videos almost exclusively humiliate men (though straight-up "bondage" movies are equal-opportunity degraders). If you've ever walked into a sex shop and seen its astounding collection of leashes, riding crops, and ball-gags, you know that this is one of the most common and best-selling fetishes out there.

> **TURN-ONS:** If pain is your pleasure, then welcome home.
>
> **TURN-OFFS:** One of the only fetishes that can lead to an emergency room visit.
>
> **SAMPLE TITLE:** *A Lady and Her Slave* (2003)

Bukkake

This Japanese export aims to turn the female face into abstract art. Literally translated as "splash," the practice involves a large group of men—often one hundred or more—taking turns ejaculating on a woman's mug (in rare cases the recipient is male). The bukkake mythos holds that the practice started in Japan's feudal period as a form of punishment for adulterous women. The offender would be tied up, and all the men of her village would take turns adding an ounce of humiliation. (Way to teach her not to fool around with other men, morons.) Today's bukkake girls are willing—even enthusiastic—recipients of the Jackson Pollack treatment.

TURN-ONS: Do you like to fast-forward from climax to climax? Heaven awaits.

TURN-OFFS: You may never enjoy a cruller again.

SAMPLE TITLE: *American Bukkake* (1999)

Chubby

"Chubby" denotes a slight paunch—that spare tire or flabby backside most of us battle at some point. The stars of this genre don't quite fit that description. Some are considerably overweight. Most are clinically obese. A typical chubby video will pair a trim (even bony) man with a large woman for some deliciously disproportionate sex. One movie even puts 420- and 370-pound women in the boxing ring to battle it out in bikinis. See? Porn is a buffet—there's something for everyone (some foods are just a little higher in calories than others).

TURN-ONS: If you get aroused looking at "before" pictures, then by all means.

TURN-OFFS: Cottage cheese aplenty.

SAMPLE TITLE: *Chunky Hallow's Eve* (2003)

Creampie

Also known as "internal" movies, I'm sad to report that they have very little to do with pastries. Actually, *nothing* to do with pastries. For a porno to fall under the "creampie" umbrella it has to meet three criteria: First, the penis must be firmly ensconced in an orifice below the waist. Second, the man (or *men*—sometimes up to five in a row) must ejaculate *inside* a partner rather than pulling out. Finally, the partner must then expel the wretched results for all the world to see. There are several different methods of doing this, each harder to describe than the last.

TURN-ONS: For some, it's a welcome alternative to porn's typical "draw and fire" approach.

TURN-OFFS: It's the "expel" phase of the operation that's tough to watch—especially if you have your TV's volume turned up.

SAMPLE TITLE: *Choc Full A Nut* (2003)

Double Penetration

"DP" (as it's affectionately known) is the act of penetrating a woman's "good" and "bad" places at the same time. This is usually accomplished by two studs (or a stud and a strap-on, or any other variant you can dream up). Therefore, students, "triple penetration" occurs when all *three* of a woman's orifices are simultaneously occupied. Now, don't make the mistake of confusing "double penetration" with "double anal." "Double anal" requires that two penises occupy the same anus. The same distinction must be made between "triple penetration" and "triple anal." Class dismissed.

TURN-ONS: Mathematically speaking, it's twice the value of single penetration.

TURN-OFFS: If you're into sensuality, don't get off on this floor.

SAMPLE TITLE: *One in the Pink, One in the Stink* (2004)

Feet

I know this one seems self-explanatory, but the foot fetish has so many different subgenres that I couldn't let you risk it. First up are "shrimping" (toe sucking) videos. God knows there's no shortage of girl/girl shrimping, straight shrimping, and self-shrimping titles. A bit harder to find are "foot worship" movies—first cousins to domination that usually feature men licking the high-heeled shoes of their masters. Next we have the "foot job," the most popular subgenre—covering everything from rubbing with feet to inserting them into someone else. Last and definitely least, there's "foot crushing"—close-up shots of women crushing tiny objects with their bare feet. (For more on this, see "Japan" on page 160.)

Gonzo

I know what you're thinking: There was always something strange about that Muppet. The one with the phallic, felt-covered nose and a proclivity for chasing chickens. But rest assured, porn's most popular genre is not named after "The Great Gonzo" of your youth. In fact, the name comes from Hunter S. Thompson's self-described style of subjective (albeit drug-induced) journalism. "Gonzo" refers to the *style* in which pornos are made, not the kind of sex they offer. Most are plot-less, micro-budgeted vehicles where the man doing the filming might very well be the man doing the humping. In *all* gonzo, the per-formers are free to acknowledge the camera, and the director is often heard barking orders in the background. The vast majority of pornos produced today fall into the gonzo category.

TURN-ONS: They waste no time get-ting down to business.

TURN-OFFS: There's very little that doesn't make the final cut—including shots of fat crew guys picking their noses. Bye-bye, erection!

SAMPLE TITLE: *Gluteus to the Maximus* (2001)

Hentai

Another export from the isle of gadgets and giggles. This one translates to "per-verted," and it describes the adults-only cartoons that have made Japanimation virtually synonymous with smut. Hentai goes further than most porn is willing to (and *able* to—since it has the distinct advantage of being drawn). There are hun-dreds of these films on the market, but in the interest of saving you time and money, I humbly present the plot of every hentai film ever made: A teen waif with huge breasts and blue (maybe pink) hair arrives at a new school. She's never been touched beneath her snugly fitting uniform, but all that changes when her (equally hot and giant-eyed) room-mate seduces her in the shower. Soon she's sliding down more poles than a fireman, until some-how a witch (or mummy, or alien) traps her and violates her with its twenty tentacles. But wait! It's all a dream. She wakes up, virginal as ever . . . or is she?

TURN-ONS: Cartoons and graphic sex, together at last.

TURN-OFFS: A sixty-minute movie is usually fifty-seven minutes of poorly dubbed dialogue and three minutes of weird penetrations.

SAMPLE TITLE: *Immoral Sisters* (2002)

Hot Rod

Most guys love sex and most guys love cars—so it's only natural that someone eventually found a way to combine the two. "Hot rod" titles feature couples having sex in, on, and around the hottest whips on the blacktop. And the box covers often hype the cars more than they do the girls. Potential buyers are enticed by the promise of "1965 Chevy Corvette" and "1997 Dodge Viper." They're also barraged with an endless stream of car-related innuendos like, "These girls know how to drive stick!" and "These girls take it up the tailpipe!" Besides the automotive backdrops, there's very little to distinguish the sex in this genre from any other—but "if you love wheels and heels, then this is where the rubbers hit the road!"

> **TURN-ONS:** I suppose it beats watching hot rods without the sex.
>
> ---
>
> **TURN-OFFS:** Do we really need to combine our porn with other hobbies to make it watchable? Has it come to that?
>
> ---
>
> **SAMPLE TITLE:** *Sweet Rides* (1999)

Little People

Don't bother looking for the "little people" section at your local adult video store. Pornos prefer the decidedly un-PC "midget" to describe anyone of short stature. Midget movies have been around since the classic era, offering all the hard-core sex (and twice the stepladders) of their full-sized counterparts. There are little studs with full-sized women, little women with full-sized studs, and (less often) little people with each other. As you'd expect, these movies tend to be degrading, even by porn standards. You'll find little people dressed like Oompa Loompas, women carried around in suitcases, and men wearing diapers and sucking pacifiers. You'll also find performer names that overstate the obvious, like "Bridget the Midget," "Gidget the Midget," and "Twiget the Midget." Film titles range from the stupid (*Dial M for Midget*) to the gag-inducing (*Pee Midget Pee*).

> **TURN-ONS:** Makes men with average-sized penises feel like John Holmes.
>
> ---
>
> **TURN-OFFS:** Unlike other genres, midget movies can backfire—leaving you depressed rather than turned on.
>
> ---
>
> **SAMPLE TITLE:** *Double Midgetation* (2000)

Mature

Well-behaved porn? Nope. Porn that's wise beyond it years? Try again. In this case, "mature" is a euphemism for "old," as in "senior citizens," as in "senior citizens bumping uglies." So much for growing old gracefully. The sexual relics portrayed here are almost always women—women who could tie their impossibly wrinkled mammaries in a knot if they so desired. These old souls are teamed up with men young enough to be their grandchildren. And yes, they do everything their younger counterparts do. Call them nursing home nymphos, call them social security sluts—come to think of it, call them a *doctor*.

TURN-ONS: Everyone needs a break from supple, young flesh now and then . . . I guess . . .

TURN-OFFS: Think imagining your grandma getting tag-teamed is bad? Try watching it.

SAMPLE TITLE: *Drop Your Panties Granny* (1999)

Pony Play

Apparently, "regular" bondage and domination is too pedestrian for some. "Pony play" has nothing to do with actual horses (thank you, God) but it allows men and women to *become* horses. There's a very specific set of rules. For instance, once you've assumed the role of pony, speaking is forbidden unless absolutely necessary. For hours at a time, you're expected to do *everything* a pony would do—nibble carrots, poop on the ground, and whinny when your "master" fondles your pony parts. There's also a suggested wardrobe: shiny black shoes (just like hooves!), harnesses, plumes, and butt plugs with horse tails attached to them. "Ponies" are usually hitched to carts or wagons (which they pull in public, where legal), but bareback riding is also acceptable. If you happen to run across a riding club, tell them to "quit horsing around." They LOVE it!

TURN-ONS: Who doesn't love ponies?

TURN-OFFS: These aren't ponies. They're people wearing butt plugs and blinders.

SAMPLE TITLE: *Fetish and Magic 3* (2003)

Pro-Am

Here are pornos even *you* could star in. "Pro-ams" are "professional/amateur" movies that pair "ordinary, everyday" people with experienced porn stars. (The term actually originated in sports—you'll find pro-am competitions in sports like golf and bass fishing.) In porn, you'll usually find a cameraman/stud approaching women in public and asking them if they'd like to make a quick buck. If the answer is "yes," then it's onto his nearby apartment for some poorly filmed sex. In another variation, a husband or boyfriend is paid to watch his woman rub middles with a stranger. The mid-'90s saw a new kind of pro-am emerge in the form of the extreme gang bang. Today, professional starlets routinely take on *hundreds* of wanna-be woodsmen at a time.

TURN-ONS: Watching average-looking people humiliate themselves for a few dollars.

TURN-OFFS: Watching average-looking people humiliate themselves for a few dollars.

SAMPLE TITLE: *Up 'n Cummers* (1993)

Scat

I can't stress this enough: These are *not* films about the golden age of jazz. The name is derivative of "scatological," or "the study of fecal excrement." To put it another way: By the time these movies are over, the performers look like they were in a fudge shop during the blitzkrieg. Let me also be clear: I hate this stuff. HATE it. Watching one of these films is like watching a commercial for the end of the world. Even so, I support your right to see people become willing human toilets. Scat movies usually feature all the sex acts you'll find in a "normal" porno—the only difference being that everyone's covered in shit. For those with strong enough gag reflexes and a burning curiosity to see depravity at its most depraved, you have a challenge ahead. These films are almost impossible to find in any self-respecting adult shop.

TURN-ONS: Nothing.

TURN-OFFS: Everything.

SAMPLE TITLE: If you really want to find this stuff, you'll find it.

Smoking

Ever feel like porn puts too much emphasis on penetration and not enough on emphysema? Apparently some of you do, as evidenced by the popularity of this unlikely genre. "Smoking" movies are usually a series of naked women puffing on cigarettes by themselves. The action "heats up" when they use their coffin nails to masturbate, or (in some cases) smoke them with their vaginas. Some scenes feature a pair of women blowing smoke on each other's naughty bits. If things get really wild, you might see a pipe or cigar between their lips. Generally speaking, there are no men to be found, and there's no penetration taking place. Just smoking. Lots and lots of smoking.

TURN-ONS: There's a certain "1940s detective movie" sexiness to a woman with a cigarette.

TURN-OFFS: Surgeon General's Warning: This fetish may be linked with stupidity.

SAMPLE TITLE: *For My Smokey Boy* (1999)

Squirting

A genre beset with controversy, not because it's particularly offensive—but because some people think it's a hoax. Do women really make *stuff* when they climax? The existence of "squirting" (another way of saying "female ejaculation") was debated by the sexologists of the mid-twentieth century. More recent studies have shown that the majority of women (up to 75 percent) do secrete a semen-like protein when they achieve orgasm—but in such tiny amounts that it'd be undetectable to the naked eye. That's a big difference from the "squirt queens" of porn, who could fill bathtubs with the fluid they produce. So what gives? The truth is, when you're watching a porn star "squirt," you're probably watching her *pee*. In a handful of women, the muscle contractions that come with an orgasm lead to a loss of bladder control. If you're the kind of person who looks at a lawn sprinkler and wishes it was wearing eyeshadow, you'll have no trouble finding these movies. There are hundreds of titles (not to mention entire websites) devoted to squirting; even stars (see Annie Sprinkle, page 72) who've become famous because of their inability to hold it in.

TURN-ONS: At least you know they're not faking it.

TURN-OFFS: Is incontinence a turn-on?

SAMPLE TITLE: *Gusher Girls* (2002)

Teen

Pornography offers people what they can't have in real life. And for the comb-over crowd that makes up so much of its audience, nothing's more out of reach than teenage girls. So it's no wonder that *thousands* of dirty movies highlight the word "teen" in their titles—whether there are any actual teens in the movie or not. (You may be shocked to learn that some smut peddlers play fast and loose with the truth.) It's sad to see a woman who looks old enough to have teenagers being touted as one, but it happens every day. This "over-teenification" has led at least one pornographer to have girls hold their driver's licenses up to the camera before sex. Likewise, Hustler Video's *Barely Legal* series is one of porn's best selling, in part because it finds girls who not only look young, but are. Because if there's anything worse than getting into porn, it's lying about your age.

> **TURN-ONS:** The better titles manage to find girls (and boys) before they become tattooed and implanted.
>
> **TURN-OFFS:** You have to wade through a lot of phony "teens" to find the real thing.
>
> **SAMPLE TITLE:** *Eighteen Candles* (2001)

Wrestling

It's widely accepted that any wrestling match, if allowed to go on long enough, leads to sex. "Wrestling" movies follow this logic to its messy conclusion. The mechanics are simple enough: men and women take to the mats. They oil up, grapple for a few minutes, and *presto*! Out come the genitals and a whole new definition of "choke hold." Fans of Hulk Hogan and Superfly Snuka will find little to cheer about here. The wrestling is sloppy—I have yet to see a single DDT or suplex. But if you're so competitive that even your *porn* needs winners and losers, then "llet's get ready to maaasturbaaate!!!"

> **TURN-ONS:** Xena fans, your porn awaits.
>
> **TURN-OFFS:** There's enough to worry about in the bedroom without adding a referee to the mix.
>
> **SAMPLE TITLE:** *Ranch Hand Rumble* (2001)

Okay, so now you have some options. What next? Where do you get your eager little paws on all this great stuff?

The Internet

According to Merriam-Webster, the Internet is "a worldwide system of interconnected computer networks created for the purpose of distributing pornography." All right, so maybe that's stretching the truth. But to demonstrate just how much porn is available online, I keyed the following phrases into Google and recorded the results:

★ **Clown Porn:** 6,320 pages
★ **Indian Donkey Porn:** 2 pages
★ **Elvis Porn:** 781 pages
★ **Haunted Porn:** 292 pages
★ **Canadian Porn:** 25,200 pages

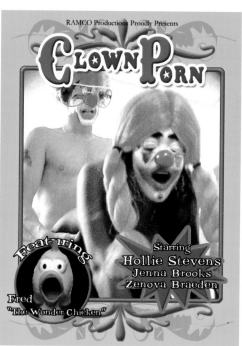

It might seem bizarre that "clown porn" generates more results than "clown school" (4,490) but consider this: Pornography was one of the Internet's first commercial applications, and remains its most profitable. There are more than 250 million Web pages devoted to porn—almost one page for every man, woman, and child in America. Most of those pages break down like this:

Pay Sites

Members pay a fee (usually around $19.95 a month) for unlimited access to picture galleries and video downloads. Some of the better pay sites belong to the porn studios and stars themselves.

THE UPSIDE: Glossy and dependable with high-quality content.

THE DOWNSIDE: $239 a year.

EXAMPLE: private.com

Free Sites

Before you get too excited, most of these "free" sites are nothing more than a collection of links to teasers—samples to con you into paying the full membership price. The key to beating the system is volume—sample enough hors d'oeuvres, and who needs dinner? Luckily, most sites update their links daily, so sample away!

THE UPSIDE: Are you kidding? It's free!

THE DOWNSIDE: The best stuff's reserved for the paying customers.

EXAMPLE: thehun.net

Rental Sites

This is why the Internet was created. You can choose a porno from thousands of titles, have it delivered to your door, watch it, and return it—all without seeing or speaking to another human being. And no late fees! It's the masturbating agoraphobic's dream come true.

THE UPSIDE: Anonymity, convenience, and selection.

THE DOWNSIDE: Terrible for your tan.

EXAMPLE: wantedlist.com

Portals

Some of the best porn sites aren't really porn sites at all. They're gateways: humor, news, or pop culture pages that just happen to feature tons of dirty videos, pictures, and links to porn affiliates—proving once again that there's only one way to make money on the Internet.

THE UPSIDE: Less likely to get you busted by the office IT guy.

THE DOWNSIDE: Some pages also post images of death and dismemberment.

EXAMPLE: stileproject.com

Auction Sites

Thanks to the anonymity of eBay, people are starting to unload their old porn at bargain-basement prices. Maybe they're moving in with a girlfriend. Maybe they're joining a cult. Who cares why? One's man's trash is another man's treasure. Auction sites are great for tracking down those hard-to-find classics and non-movie memorabilia.

THE UPSIDE: You'll often find entire porno collections up for sale, if you're the type of person who does all their Christmas shopping in one day.

THE DOWNSIDE: God only knows what kind of pervert you'll be dealing with.

EXAMPLE: eBay.com

Adult Bookstores

Chances are there's one in your backyard. Some twenty-five-thousand adult bookstores do business in the United States. That's nearly eight for every county and parish, and more than enough for every city and town to have one of its own. "Bookstore" is a bit of a misnomer—you'll find precious little to read in most of these shops. What you will find:

★ **Movies:** Mostly newer "gonzo" titles sold at eye-popping prices. You're better off buying online.

★ **Sex Toys and Accessories:** The bread and butter of the modern-day bookstore. Dildos of all shapes and sizes, lubrication by the ounce or gallon, "working" rubber replicas of your favorite porn starlet's anatomy, and so much more.

★ **Peep Shows:** Their prime is long gone, but a number of operational booths still exist. Some play video clips; others let you watch a flesh-and-blood stripper through a pane of glass.

Unfortunately, there's also a high probability that you'll encounter:

★ **Creeps:** There always seems to be a mousy middle-aged man with thick glasses and a Members Only jacket, endlessly browsing while dabbing the sweat off his brow. Can't blame him, though. Beats talking to the cats all day in mom's wood-paneled basement.

★ **Moans and Groans:** If your local adult bookstore is equipped with a peep show booth (hell, even if it's not), you may be subjected to the occasional muffled "yeah" or "oh."

★ **Someone You Know:** Whether you live in a metropolis or a one-horse town, chances are you'll run into a friend, coworker, or pastor sooner or later. Start preparing those excuses.

Newsstands

It's one of the joys of living in a major metropolis: the ability to walk to any street corner or subway station and buy a newspaper, a lottery ticket, and *Balloon Butts Monthly* from the same old man.

Independent Video Stores

The most offensive thing at your local Blockbuster is probably the Jennifer Lopez shelf. Corporate chains don't cater to porn watchers. But curtained-off corners are a proud tradition of the neighborhood video stores that sprang up in the '70s and '80s. In order to stay afloat, they offer what the big boys can't: Cult, Kung-Fu, Gore, Blaxploitation, and of course, Adult. They also offer employees who know a thing or two about movies (including smut) and can point you in the right direction. Some stores even let you trade in your old pornos for new ones. A few fine examples from around the country:

★ Casa Video (Tucson, AZ)
★ Pedazo Chunk (Austin, TX)
★ Rocket Video (Los Angeles, CA)
★ Roscoe Video (Independence, MO)
★ Scarecrow Video (Seattle, WA)
★ TLA Video (Philadelphia, PA)
★ World of Video (New York, NY)

The Kinsey Institute

Housed at Indiana University, the institute is named for the late Alfred C. Kinsey (1894–1956), arguably the greatest sexual behaviorist of the twentieth century. Today's students and researchers of sex, gender, and reproduction have a powerful tool at their disposal—the world's biggest collection of porn. Consider:

★ 12,000 adult films and videos from 1915 to present
★ 7,000 sexual artifacts from around the world (some more than two thousand years old)
★ 48,000 adult images from 1870 to present

And more dirty books and magazines than you could read in a lifetime. But don't buy that plane ticket just yet. Tours are offered only once a month, and access to the institute's collection is restricted.

The Vatican (?)

Some conspiracy theorists maintain that the Vatican has been snatching up erotica and locking it away since the Renaissance. Father Leonard Boyle, the Vatican's chief librarian from 1984 to 1998, denied ever seeing any in the Church's vast collections. Somebody get me Oliver Stone.

Every weekday, when the clock strikes midnight, the glass slipper comes off and Cinemax turns into a slutty little stepsister. The Sandra Bullock movies disappear, replaced by *Forbidden Sins*, *Deviant Vixens*, *Naked Lies*, and *Human Desires*. All bumping, all grinding, all night long. Officially speaking, this is "Cinemax After Dark." To everyone else, it's "Skinemax," America's premier outlet for soft-core porn.

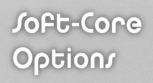

Soft-Core Options

"Soft-core" is porn that doesn't feature close-ups of penetration. A kind of "porn-lite"—rented in mainstream video stores, ordered in hotel rooms, and broadcast on late-night cable or satellite channels. There are two distinct groups of soft-core movies. First you have the "trims." Hard-core pornographers almost always edit "soft" versions of their movies in hopes of reaching a wider audience and reaping more profits. Second, you have made-to-order soft-core (most of the fare on "Skinemax" falls into this category). The budgets are bigger (often in the $500,000 to $1,000,000 range), and you'll even find a few Hollywood has-beens baring it all for a paycheck. But that doesn't change the fact that the films are *awful*.

Like their full-penetration cousins, soft-core movies are full of recycled plots, terrible dialogue, and high school drama club acting. Generally speaking, the sex is simulated—actors rub pelvises on red satin sheets and moan over synthesized soundtracks. The results are (unintentionally) hilarious—women thrusting their asses against their partners' belly buttons; men doing their best to "sell" the climax. Sure, there's plenty of full-frontal nudity, but who wants R-rated porn?

Apparently, the answer is "plenty of people." Cinemax has no plans to scale back its soft-core programming. Almost every cable and satellite provider offers soft-core on a pay-per-view basis. And according to ABC News, nearly 80 percent of all programming ordered in hotel rooms is . . . that's right . . . soft-core porn.

When *Deep Throat* took America by storm in 1972, it was acceptable (even chic) to be spotted in line. *Throat*-goers included luminaries like Truman Capote, Warren Beatty, and even *Tonight Show* sidekick Ed McMahon. But that was decades ago. These days, celebrities face far-reaching, even career-ending consequences for being caught in a stroke house. Just ask Paul Reubens, a.k.a. Pee-wee Herman.

On July 26, 1991, Reubens was in his hometown of Sarasota, Florida, visiting his

Pee-Wee's Pornhouse

parents. Production of *Pee-wee's Playhouse* had recently ended, and he was looking forward to some well-deserved R&R. The long-haired, goateed Reubens found what he was looking for at the South Trail XXX Cinema, which was hosting a triple feature. Unbeknownst to Reubens, it was also hosting a vice squad sting operation. During a screening of *Nancy Nurse*, he was arrested for allegedly exposing himself to an undercover officer. When the press caught wind of the story, all hell broke loose in Pee-wee Land. CBS pulled reruns of *Playhouse* off the air. Stores pulled Pee-wee merchandise off the shelves. There were even (false) reports that his star on the Hollywood Walk of Fame had been jackhammered. He pleaded no contest to a charge of indecent exposure, paid $85 in court costs, a $50 fine, and agreed to film an anti-drug public service announcement. In return, the charge was removed from his criminal record.

It would be harder to remove from the public's memory. The Pee-wee character made only one more appearance after the Sarasota incident (at the 1991 MTV Video Music Awards, where he opened with "Heard any good jokes lately?"). In recent interviews, Reubens has hinted at a Pee-wee comeback, but restoring his image won't be easy. Try a Google image search for "Pee-wee Herman" and see how many times this mug shot pops up.

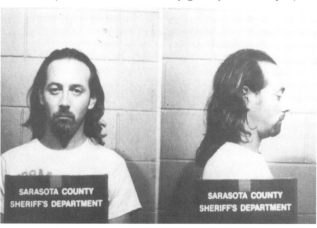

SARASOTA COUNTY SHERIFF'S DEPARTMENT

SARASOTA COUNTY SHERIFF'S DEPARTMENT

I envy the porn lovers of tomorrow. They'll experience smut in ways we dare not imagine—through holograms, "fully functional" robots, and implanted memories. Spurred by the misery of their lonely, sexless lives, porn's brightest scientists and engineers are working around the clock to develop new and exciting ways to get off. A few of them have already arrived:

The Virtual Sex Machine

"As it happens on the screen . . . it happens to YOU!" So proclaims the company behind The Virtual Sex Machine, a motorized tube that fits over the penis (no word on when the women's version will be available) and attaches to your computer. Pop in one of the VSM-compatible CD-ROMs, and away you go! Your alter ego looks down at his penis while a lady (of your choosing) performs just about any act imaginable. Whenever *he's* touched, *you* feel it. Just like Elliott and E.T.!

X-Vision 3-D Porn

The X-Vision software and wireless glasses turn your computer's monitor into a 3-D movie theater—a fact that's made it a "must-have" with tech-savvy masturbation enthusiasts. The system makes your monitor switch between left-eye and right-eye views at undetectably high speeds. The glasses flicker in sync with the monitor, fooling your horny brain into thinking those 2-D appendages are right in front of your face. Sucker!

Interactive CD-ROMs

Once heralded as the greatest porno-vation since waxing, dirty CD-ROMs seem to have gone the way of the Backstreet Boys. The concept was outstanding—point and click your way through a sexual adventure in the privacy of your home office. You chose the partner, picked the positions, and controlled the pace. Some discs even provided headsets for voice-activated commands. Unfortunately, the execution never lived up to the expectations. The stories were garbled messes with pitiful payoffs, and the video looked like it was transmitted from a deep-space probe. The interactive movement is still alive, though. DVDs like Digital Playground's *Virtual Sex With . . .* series allow viewers to control their favorite stars through a first-person interface. Who knows what other innovations tomorrow will bring?

An Ode to Times Square

Once it was the dirtiest, scariest part of New York City. A little slice of Sodom and Gomorrah between 6th and 9th Avenues (east to west) and 39th and 52nd Streets (north to south). By the time Longacre Square was renamed in 1904, it already had a reputation for vice. It did that reputation proud for most of the twentieth century—playing home to streetwalkers and porno theaters, and surviving repeated cleanup attempts. Mayor Rudolph Giuliani finally succeeded in the 1990s, clearing the way for the square as it is today: a tourist-friendly collection of toy stores, TV studios, and family restaurants. In a way, the story of Times Square is the story of porn itself—once dodgy and deviant, now corporate and controlled. It's a story best expressed through the gift of poetry.

Every New Year's Eve they drop
a ball with sparkling lights on top.
But once upon an old Times Square,
balls were dropping everywhere.

Vaudeville follies, cabaret,
hookers serving straight and gay.
Dirty films for all to see
at Venus, Eros, and Capri.

Hustlers, pimps, and sex on stages.
Peep show booths and girls in cages.
Stabbings, shootings, garbage piles,
sidewalks strewn with old crack vials.

All the pornos being sold!
All the vices to behold!
Women working through the night,
not a single badge in sight.

But wait, what's this—a Disney store?
Why, that's no place to find a whore!
Where are all my God fanatics,
platinum wigs, and strung-out addicts?

Lo! It's home to MTV,
Toys R' Us, and Applebee's!
A theater once so full of sex?
Just another multiplex!

Oh square, oh square! Look what
they've done!
The girls have fled, the pimps have run!
They've made you safe and clean and
bright—an awful place to spend the
night.

5

it's a smut world, after all

Most of the porn we've dealt with thus far has been made in America. And why not? The United States is the world's leading peddler of adult entertainment. But it's by no means the *only* superpower in the skin game. There are six billion potential porn-lovers on this planet, and 95 percent of them aren't American. Good God! How do they cope? Hop aboard my private yacht, *The Skank of the Seas*, and I'll show you. We'll sail the globe in search of new and exotic porn—hitting all but one continent (my publisher wouldn't spring for a trip to Antarctica) and recording the strange customs of the natives. We'll see how they manage without an $11 billion-dollar porn industry in their backyard. We'll even learn some potentially life-saving travel tips. But above all, we'll be reminded of that special bond that all humans share regardless of nationality—horniness.

Real shame about Antarctica, though. I hear they're *filthy* down there.

With the wind at my back, I set a course for porn. And though I couldn't know it at the time, my ship and her crew were about to encounter more sex than *The Love Boat* ever dreamed. I've done my best to chronicle the strange and exciting customs of each country. In retrospect, it probably would've been more time- and cost-efficient if we hadn't visited them in alphabetical order.

Afghanistan

Under the brutal Taliban regime, Afghanistan was anything but a porn lover's paradise. Would you be turned on in a country where premarital sex is punishable by death? But after the Taliban went bye-bye, Afghans suddenly found themselves with new and unprecedented freedoms. Some of the first visible changes (besides a drastic reduction in beard lengths) were the satellite dishes that started popping up on rooftops—dishes receiving *hundreds* of uncensored channels from the West. One of the most popular premium channels? 100% Hardcore. You'll also find pirated pornos for sale in the video stores of Kabul (mostly imports form Pakistan and India). Keep in mind: This is a country where until recently, women were publicly beaten for showing so much as an ankle.

Australia

All "down under" jokes aside, the Land of Oz is home to a thriving porn industry, although much of it is owned by Americans. Therefore, it's no surprise that Aussie pornos and American pornos are largely identical. The only visible difference seems to be a bit more "overgrowth" in the bush country. Also, the Australian government has stricter decency standards than the United States. Its Office of Film and Literature Classification is a citizen panel charged with reviewing and rating every piece of filmed entertainment. Ironic, then, that most of the country's pornos are shot in its capital, Canberra. Some fetishes are off limits (you won't find any peeing or spanking movies), and in many parts of the country it's illegal for sex shops to carry pornos—so mail order thrives. The Outback even has its own Jenna Jameson–esque superstar, Jodie Moore.

Brazil

A country that knows how to get its freak on. A country of nipple-riffic carnivals, topless beaches, and yes, dirty movies galore. But even though Brazil's porn industry is estimated to be the second largest in the world, HIV testing isn't mandatory for its performers. Instead, there's an "unwritten agreement" that men have to

Brazil:
And now, we are proud to present the Solid Gold Dancers.

Afghanistan:
By Taliban standards, *this* is pornography

use condoms (about 80 percent actually do). Rather than blame pornography for the spread of the disease (a very fashionable position elsewhere in the world) the Brazilian government has started to hand out movies that feature condom use to raise the level of safe-sex awareness. The government also required that all porn come with a warning label urging people to use protection.

Canada

Canadians have a nasty reputation for being a polite, law-abiding people. So it's surprising to learn that the home of the Mounties is also home to a thriving hard-core industry. If anything, Canadians are more sexually open than their American neighbors. Satellite provider BEV offers several channels of full-penetration programming to its Canadian customers, and Montreal ranks with Los Angeles's San Fernando Valley in terms of porno production. Montreal is also home to some of the most innovative content on the Web, like *Pornstar Académie*—a contest where average men and women are "trained" to become fully functional porn stars. However, it's not all fun and games. In 1992, the Canadian Supreme Court ruled that "degrading" and "dehumanizing" films were not protected by free speech laws. This has resulted in the banning and confiscating of pornos that feature BDSM, golden showers, and other fetishes deemed too extreme.

Denmark

In 1969, Denmark became the first country to legalize all forms of pornography. The following year, it reported a decline in the number of reported sex offenses. Things have been looking up ever since. Like their Scandinavian neighbors, the Danes are a cold chillin' bunch—they don't care if you're straight or gay, clothed or topless, man or beast. That's not to say they're tolerant of everything. According to Danish law, you have to be eighteen to appear in a porno (but only sixteen to buy one). Dirty movies are even offered to nursing home residents. Hey, why the hell not? Prostitution was officially legalized in 1999, and there are some six thousand men and women on the job today. One Danish company even offers its employees free subscriptions to porn sites (so long as they don't surf during office hours).

Does Pornography Lead to Social Decay?

Porn has been legal and widely available in Denmark for decades. Here are some of the ill effects:

★ An extremely low crime rate

★ The second-highest per-capita income in Europe

★ No real poverty

★ An HIV-positive population of 0.2 percent (compared to 0.6 percent in the United States)

★ Free health care and education for every citizen

★ Declining interest in pornography (most porn in Denmark is sold to visiting foreigners)

France

France's attitude toward pornography is captured by Andrew Hussey in an article for the British magazine *New Statesman*. Hussey writes that the French have become worried about *la mal baise*, "bad sex that is offensive because it's, well, not really dirty enough." France has always been ahead of the sexual-maturity curve—after all, its blush-proof attitude is a matter of national pride. Nudity is ubiquitous, and pornography is more widely accepted and available here than just about anywhere else in the world. Mainstream Canal Plus TV features a monthly porn magazine show called *Le Journal du Hard*, and the annual Hot d'Or Festival (which awards porno excellence around the world) threatens to steal the spotlight from Cannes every year.

France: Showing off at the Hot d'Or Festival.

Porn employs more than twelve thousand people in Southern California, and the overwhelming majority work in Los Angeles's San Fernando Valley (the side of the hill that the Hollywood sign turns its back to). Most of the industry's biggest companies are headquartered here, and most of its biggest stars either live in or run

their fanclubs from Valley towns like Chatsworth, Van Nuys, and Canoga Park. Some ten thousand adult movies are produced here every year (far more than anywhere else in the world), pumping billions into the California economy.

California's San Fernando Valley: Center of the Known Porn Universe

The Valley was home to about five thousand Native Americans when Europeans first arrived in 1769. By the 1780s, cattle farmers were using those same Native Americans as cheap labor (and turning big profits). The Valley remained cattle country for almost

another century before making the transition to wheat farming in the 1860s. This "home on the range" vibe stuck around through the 1950s and '60s—a time when the Valley was used for filming westerns (shucks, Roy Rogers and Dale Evans even *lived* there).

In the early '80s, home video was booming, and the porn industry was relocating from San Francisco to Los Angeles. The Valley offered producers a perfect place to settle down. But why? Was it the metaphoric significance of working (literally) in the shadow of Hollywood? The nudity-friendly warm weather? Good Lord, no. It was the dirt-cheap real estate. Like the cattle farmers before them, today's porn giants are using the Valley's low costs to turn big profits. Companies like Vivid, Metro, VCA, Wicked, Digital Playground, Pure Play, and Red Light District are all headquartered mere minutes from each other—in some cases, across the street from each other.

Germany

German porn has more poop flying around than the primate house at the Berlin Zoo. The adult industry is saturated with "Natursekt" films—scatological nightmares of pee-drinking, feces-smearing, even feces-eating. Your humble author has actually seen a man and woman "Lady and the Tramp" a piece of brown badness. On top of all that, poop has its own cute German nickname—Kaviar (for "caviar"). I'm no psychologist, but when you name a turd after a delicacy, Prozac ain't gonna make a dent, my friend. Now, if I were a journalist, objectivity would compel me to report that Deutschland also has plenty of "vanilla" porn and that it's more than a nation of toilet-worship and fine automobiles. Luckily, I'm not a journalist. So here are a few more examples from the land of blondes and bratwurst:

★ **Uromania:** If Natursekt films are the main course, these are the appetizers. They're strictly voyeuristic romps—scenes of men and women peeing here, there, and everywhere. Usually on each other.

★ **Fisting:** When it comes to testing the limits of human orifices, the Germans are second to none. Fisting is extremely popular in German porn, often added as a component in extreme bondage movies. I say "extreme" because we're not talking about fuzzy pink handcuffs and blindfolds here—we're talking about suspending women from the ceiling by their nipple rings.

★ **Schwanger:** "Pregnant" movies. Yes, these exist in other countries, but where else will you find pregnant women attempting to answer that age-old question: "How many carrots and pool balls can I fit in my vagina at once?"

★ **Familie and Inzest:** The idea of "keeping it in the family" is bigger in Germany than anywhere else in the world. But unlike the incest films of other countries, these go to the extremes of showing a father smearing feces on his daughter and a brother fisting his sister. (Sorry, aspiring musicians—the band name "Fisted Sister" is already taken. It's a metal group based in Dublin.)

Israel

The holy land is a schizophrenic blend of progressive Westernism and religious conservatism. On one hand, the Playboy Channel is extremely popular; on the other, so is protesting against the Playboy Channel. For better or worse, porn is alive and well in the Middle East's beacon of democracy. For better if you like your sex with an extra helping of guilt. For worse because Israel is home to the vilest, most indefensible, and disturbing fetish I've yet to encounter—Holocaust porn. No joke. All the horrors of the concentration camps are reenacted in grainy black-and-white photos: women packed onto railcars—their heads shaven, their bodies emaciated. Tortured in ways too detestable to describe, forced to pleasure their Nazi captors, and then "killed." It's all staged, of course. But here's the worst part: The actors, distributors, and buyers of Holocaust porn are mostly Israeli. Talk about your self-hating Jews.

Italy

In most countries, porn is counterculture. In Italy, porn is simply another *part* of culture—no more taboo than linguini or opera. A recent survey showed that 37 percent of Italian women regularly watch porn on TV. This widespread tolerance has allowed Italian porn to flourish, and it's led the government to ask for its cut of the action. A measure that would have imposed a heavy tax on pornography was voted down—but only after some of the country's biggest adult film stars threatened to organize protest rallies. Why would the government cave to pressure from porn stars? Maybe because one of them served in its Parliament. Italian porn legend Cicciolina was elected to national office after running on a strong platform of: (1) Showing her breasts at every campaign stop; and (2) Proposing an initiative to ease international tensions: "I am available to make love with Saddam Hussein to achieve peace in the Middle East." After serving her two-year term, she returned to adult films. Now *that's* what I call serving your country.

Japan

I owe the German people an apology. Germany, I mocked you for being into eccentricities like poop-eating and sister-fisting. It was wrong, and I'm sorry. Even at your weirdest, you're unbearably dull compared to these guys.

The Japanese have a Jekyll-and-Hyde love affair with porn. On the surface, they're polite to a fault. But beneath that taciturn exterior, you won't find a more experimental, enthusiastic bunch of fetishists. Their porn ranges from the weird (girls drinking tons of water and struggling to control their bladders in public places) to the unwatchable (people gagging themselves and vomiting into each other's mouths during sex).

It's a country that had no enforceable laws against child pornography until the 1990s. A country that places a premium on female submissiveness (one of my favorite hypocrisies: Japanese men can get off watching women bound, gagged, and whipped, but the sight of another man's penis is so abhorrent that most Japanese pornos blur them out). We've already covered a couple Japanese originals: hentai and bukkake (see pages 130 and 133). But I'm afraid those were merely the tip of the bizarro-berg. There are more Japanese fetishes than could possibly be covered in this entire book, but here are a few of my favorites.

(Special thanks to Steven at the *Tokyo Damage Report* for making me aware of some of these oddities. You can read the *TDR* online for lots more on the weirdness of Japanese culture—fetishes and all. He also braved Tokyo's after-hours scene to bring us these pictures.)

★ **Buru-Sera ("Bloomer Sailor"):** The Japanese love a woman in uniform, so long as she's under the age of fourteen. "Sailor" refers to the look of the outfits typically worn by schoolgirls. Outfits that are available for anyone to buy—in vending machines. Also available in vending machines? Soiled schoolgirl panties. Many come complete with a certificate featuring a bio of the girl who personally soiled them for you. But wait, there's more! You can send away for a vial of schoolgirl's urine, or even—so help me—purchase individual pubic hairs from real schoolgirls. They run about $9 apiece, if you need to know.

Japan: A Bura-Sera vending machine.

★ **Foot Crush:** Here's an interesting business model. Step 1: Build silly-looking replicas of city streets, living rooms, the Capitol in Washington D.C., et cetera. Step 2: Film close-ups of women stomping on the models (with heels or bare feet). Step 3: Distribute and rake in the cash. Don't believe it? Google "foot crush" and see for yourself.

★ **Nose Torture:** The erotic art of sticking your fingers in a woman's nose and pulling upward to cause her pain. Occasionally the use of tiny nose clamps and leashes is acceptable.

★ **Patience Face:** "Patience Face" places women in giant boxes so only their heads are visible. Inside the box, men "do their business." But we (the audience) never see that—all *we* see is her face . . . sometimes for two straight hours.

★ **Chin-Chin (A cute way of saying "penis"):** A man approaches "everyday" women on the street and gives them a health class–style lecture on the penis. He then takes the women inside and continues the lecture using a live model.

★ **Meri Fetchi ("Wet Fetish"):** Women sitting naked in a bathtub or swimming pool. Just sitting, mind you. Alone. That's it. That's the fetish.

★ **Skatto ("Scat"):** Westerners affectionately call it "Japscat." Take all of the urine and excrement of German Natursekt movies, throw in a healthy dose of puke, and voilà!

★ **Mutant Love:** Drawings of naked girls with serious (but sexy!) deformities—ten breasts, eyes next to their vaginas, and yes, even *vaginas* next to their vaginas.

The Netherlands

Any nation with a city like Amsterdam is all right by me. Steeped in history, lined with centuries-old buildings, and teeming with sightseeing cyclists, you'd never think this was the most sexually liberal place on earth. But walk into any of the countless adult shops in the city's famed Red Light District and it becomes clear that you're not in Kansas anymore. With the exception of child porn, the Dutch will sell you movies featuring just about anything—farm animals and all. Peep show booths remain popular here, as do live sex shows, but it's the brothels that really make this the ultimate destination for sexually adventurous travelers. They're everywhere—shops with girls dancing in the windows, advertising rates and specialties. In fact, not only is prostitution legal, it's regulated by the government to ensure safety and quality. One word of advice, though: don't try to photograph the "window girls"—it's considered very bad form, and it's liable to get your camera tossed in a canal.

North Korea

Despite an abundance of theories (he's a lunatic; he's a genius) and rumors (he owns the world's biggest porn collection), very little is known about North Korean dictator Kim Jong Il. Officially, his communist government doesn't tolerate dirty movies, though it's hard to imagine anyone owning a computer or DVD player in a country that's seen millions starve since the 1990s. However, there are indications that the pudgy dictator (who's rumored to wear four-inch lifts) is quite the playboy. Kenji Fujimoto, Kim's personal chef of thirteen years, fled North Korea and published a memoir in 2003. In it, Fujimoto describes "pleasure parties" filled with naked, dancing women known as the "entourage of delight." Personal chefs and private harems? Color me a communist!

Russia

It's the college freshman of countries—restricted for so long, truly free for the first time. And like most college freshmen, it's mercilessly abusing that freedom. The former Soviet Union is undergoing a full-blown sexual revolution, and its porn industry (which existed underground throughout the 1980s) has grown into a giant. Unfortunately, this rapid growth has been largely fueled by the Russian mafia, who've become the single biggest supplier of child pornography and prostitution in the world. International sting operations have led to arrests, but haven't been able to make much of a dent in their production or distribution.

The World's Most-Used Porno Location

Nestled in downtown Los Angeles, the Entertainium is a thirty-thousand-square-foot complex where more pornos are shot than anywhere else in the world. It's a cavernous converted warehouse where film equipment lines the halls, naked people walk casually though the corridors, and moans can be heard around every corner. Each room is dressed as a different staple of porno: there's the locker room, the doctor's office, the nightclub, and the bar, complete with pool table (I don't recommend actually playing pool on it). There are also prop rooms, a freight elevator, hair and makeup rooms, and of course—showers. In a town known for big movie studios, it's the closest thing porn has to a backlot.

South Africa

This country is embroiled in a struggle between porn purveyors and religious fundamentalists. Before the end of apartheid, the government was tough on smut. Of course, they were pretty tough on blacks, too. ACA (Africa Christian Action) is a private group that's been railing against porn for over a decade. They've also used their Web site to accuse South Africa's president of "plotting a return to the pre-Christian Paganism and Animism that afflicted Africa prior to the spread of the Gospel." A "return"? Things sound pretty bad as they are now: South Africa has the highest incidence of rape in the known world. Things have gotten so bad that some companies have begun to offer—I kid you not—*rape insurance*.

Sweden

The legal age for viewing an adult movie in Sweden is fifteen. Funny, that also appears to be the average age of its porn stars. It may be taboo elsewhere in the world, but fifteen *won't* "get you twenty" in Stockholm. Like many European countries, porn is widely available, and hard-core sex can be found on public TV (the Swedes start broadcasting it after midnight). One lawmaker even suggested *increasing* the amount of porn on television to help combat Sweden's declining population. There is one snag for the ribald visitor, however—brothels are technically illegal. I say "technically" because a 1999 law made it legal to buy—but not sell—sex. Good luck finding a loophole in that one.

Taiwan

Everything else in the world is made there, so why should pornos be the exception? They're officially banned, but Taiwan's black market is alive and well—selling domestic and foreign (mostly Japanese) smut alike. Thanks to the advent of tiny video cameras, Taiwanese men have started making "hidden camera" pornos, staking out women's bathrooms, changing rooms, spas—even hotel rooms. (Note to self: Bring anti-bugging kit on next trip to Taiwan.) Dubs of these lo-fi masterworks are sold out of vans on street corners. It's gotten so bad that stores have had to regularly sweep their dressing rooms for surveillance equipment.

Taiwan: This is what happens when governments criminalize porn.

United Kingdom

Hard-core porn was illegal in Britain until the twenty-first century. Adult videos were strictly soft-core affairs, and had to be sold in one of the country's 120 or so licensed shops (licenses run around £15,000—that's $27,000 to Yanks). Any hard-core movies were likely pirated imports or cheap underground shag-fests. But all that changed when the government relaxed its censorship standards on July 18, 2000. American pornos poured into the country overnight, and the UK's leading distributors started drawing up plans to get into production. Although penetration may now be legal, there's plenty that remains off-limits to Brits: scat, bestiality, and "violent" penetration (fists, clubs, and anything else that looks like it smarts).

HUSTLER HOLLYWOOD

United Kingdom: Larry Flynt (center) attends the opening of a Hustler store in Birmingham, England.

make your own porno

6

You've come a long way, but there's one last step before you graduate with full pornophile honors: crossing the line from viewer to doer.
It'll test all the skills you've learned up to this point (and teach you a
few new ones). It'll take courage, determination, and creativity. Oh,
and a willing partner. Is everybody over eighteen? Good. Let's get
ready to apply some knowledge. Just remember to hit "record."

First things first. You have to be schooled in the basics. Like any art form, pornos have their own set of conventions. I'm not suggesting you follow them to the letter, but you can't rebel against the rules unless you know what they are. They'll strengthen your critical eye and provide the foundation for spirited discussions with friends, coworkers, and relatives.

1. Never refer to parts of the anatomy as a "penis" or a "vagina." The preferred terminology is "cock" and "pussy," respectively.
2. Always ejaculate in plain sight, preferably on the face, as this heightens everyone's pleasure.
3. Any girl who wears glasses is hiding the fact that she's an insatiable whore.
4. Sex between two people is boring. Sex between ten people is beautiful.
5. All virgins prefer to be deflowered by middle-aged men with hairy asses and potbellies.
6. Avoid sex on a bed at all costs.
7. The anus is remarkably clean and surprisingly easy to penetrate.
8. The more massive the object, the greater the pleasure of its recipient.
9. An empty orifice is a wasted orifice.
10. All women are bisexual until their fortieth birthdays, when they become full-blown lesbians.
11. Real men shave their balls.
12. The average penis measures 11½ inches (29 cm).
13. The moment a girl turns eighteen, the brain releases a chemical that turns her into a ravenous cock-craving zombie.
14. Menstruation is a myth. So is female pubic hair.
15. Never ask before you put it there. Trust me, it's okay.
16. All aunts are sluts.
17. Doctors and nurses are only in it for the sex.
18. Nothing gets a woman hotter than painfully sloppy innuendo like "we plumbers know how to unclog a pipe."
19. If a woman comes within fifty yards of a bathtub or lit candle, she masturbates.
20. Anyone who catches two people having sex is compelled to join in.

rule #11

rule #13

rule #15

☆ idea to pre-production

"It's going to happen. I'm *really* going to do this. Okay, just breathe—just be cool. The hard part is over. The part where I decide that *I*—someone who's never directed traffic, let alone a film—am going to shoot a porno."

Congratulations. That took courage. But courage alone does not a porno director make. Anyone can put the camcorder on top of the dresser and tape himself having sex. This is different. This is going to be a *movie* (even if it only runs five minutes). "How on earth am I going to pull this off? Where am I going to get the equipment? Where am I going to get the *people*? It's not like there's a listing for "fluffer" in the yellow pages. Or is there? Oh, God . . . I'm freaking out!"

Easy there. Everything's gonna be okay, I promise. We'll take this one small step at a time—together. Lucky for you, in addition to being your porn-fessor emeritus, I also have a degree in film (like everyone else in Southern California). Before you know it, you'll be yelling "deeper!" with them best of them.

The Idea

Before you go rushing out the door to enlist your cast and crew, it's a good idea to know what it is you're trying to accomplish. In order to do that, you'll need something the professionals call an "idea." You're the director, aren't you? Well, any self-respecting director needs an idea (they usually prefer "vision," but it's more or less the same deal) to get other people excited about. This "idea" can take any number of forms: It can be something floating around in your head, something scribbled on the back of a Waffle House napkin, even something called a "script." Did I lose you with that last one?

HINT: A script's the best way to go for a few reasons

1 It lets you plan more efficiently how many people, places, and things (or "nouns," if you prefer) you'll need.

2 It offers people the illusion that you know what you're doing—even if you're vomiting every half hour with incompetent fear.

3 It gives you something to throw out the window halfway into your first hour of shooting.

The Script

When crafting your script (and let's not kid ourselves—this shouldn't take more than ten minutes), try to keep a few things in mind. *Use what's available.* If you have access to an aircraft hanger, then maybe *Amelia Airslut* is the way to go. A grocery store lends itself to *Cleanup on Aisle 69*. Remember: Wherever you shoot, there's going to be nudity (and more) taking place. Make sure the owners know what they're getting into.

Parody never fails.

You have two choices here: parody a mainstream Hollywood film or TV show, or parody the conventions of porn. Both are usually slam dunks. Lampooning a well-known movie takes the burden of coming up with a plot off your shoulders. Poking fun at porn clichés lets you feel like you're above them (you elitist prick).

Open with a "bang."

Good porn wastes no time. Grab your audience by the genitals and don't let go. It's a well-known fact that all good movies have an orgasm or an explosion in the first five minutes. *Great* movies? They have both. Give us a reason to keep watching.

Keep the sex indoors.

Be safe. Statutes on public lewdness and indecent exposure vary from town to town. If you're arrested while filming a sex scene, the best you can hope for is a speedy trial. The worst? Your hometown paper prints the incident in the police blotter; a wire service picks it up; Letterman mentions you in the monologue; you become the laughingstock of the nation; you die penniless and alone. Just stay indoors, okay?

Write good dialogue.

The worst thing porn can do is take itself seriously. Take those cheesy innuendos and run with them! Example:

First Lady: Are you always this thorough when you search a lady?

Agent Surewood: Only when I suspect there's something dangerous under her clothes.

First Lady: I could have you fired, you know. My husband's the most powerful man on earth.

Agent Surewood: There's one button he doesn't have his finger on, ma'am.

Pre-Production

Once your script (or Waffle House napkin) is in decent shape, it's time to begin "pre-production"—the phase that covers planning and organizing everything that'll go into the actual shoot. Plan more now, suffer less later.

The first chore on your list? Finding other morally ambiguous people to help you out. Let's assume one of the participants is going to be *you*. That still leaves you one person short of a good sex flick. Someone who'll have sex on-camera (for free) is that rare crossbreed of exhibitionist and terrible businessperson. They're hard to find (unless you know the right rock to look under). Yes, there are Web sites and blogs devoted to helping people with this very problem. No, I'm not telling you where, because of the legal ambiguities involved with soliciting sex over the Internet. (Have fun in Leavenworth!) Let's be honest. Most of you won't be recruiting your talent online anyway. You'll be shamelessly begging that person you share a bed with. So beg wisely:

"You're too beautiful not to film."
If you *really* sell the line, you've got a shot. If the slightest bit of insincerity appears on your face, you're done for.

"It'll make me so hot for you."
Has the benefit of being true, but tread lightly. This one could blow up in your face if she says, "You're not hot for me now?"

"We'll burn the tape after we watch it."
Of course you won't. You'll make a backup dub in the middle of the night, and then stage a ceremonial destruction to put her mind at ease. Shameless, but good.

"It'll bring us closer."
Death cry of the sexually desperate. Keep this one tucked away in your bag of mind games unless it's absolutely necessary.

If you're making a more ambitious porno, you'll need at least one crew member—someone that you and your partner will both feel comfortable having around while you play porn star. Unlike recruiting talent, this part's easy:

Ask *any* of your male friends.
Not only will they say "yes," they'll show up early and bring bagels for everybody.

Equipment Checklist

Okay. You've got the story, the talent, and the crew. Now what? It's time to round up some gear. Here's what you'll need.

Camera

Unless it's a holdover from the Reagan era, chances are your camcorder will do just fine. At press time, Mini DV is the standard porn format du jour (that'll change the minute something better comes along). Use what you have, but consider a few simple ways to make your video look a little more "pro":

★ If the camera has a "white balance" option, try balancing off pale reds and blues. This'll give the picture a slight tint (depending on the color you choose—this takes some trial and error).

★ It's better to underexpose video than to overexpose. If the picture is too bright, you run the risk of "going nuclear" (i.e., your actors' noses disappear).

★ Some cameras have a "strobe" option. Setting it at the highest speed gives your video more of a "film" look.

And if you really want to do it like the pros:

★ Shoot with two cameras for twice the options in the cutting room.

★ While filming, hook your camera up to a monitor for a better idea of how everything looks.

★ Mount an external microphone (usually called a "shotgun") on your camera for higher-quality sound. Even a $30 or $40 consumer mic is an improvement for most camcorders.

★ Turn off your camera's "auto-everything" option and live on the edge!

Extra Batteries

I know it seems obvious, but running out of battery power in the middle of your stud's big climax can be devastating to your shoot (and his ego). Run your camera off AC power whenever possible.

Wide Angle Adapter

These adapters (available at most electronics stores) fit over the existing lens and allow you to see more of the action. Better yet, they make it a lot easier to keep everything in focus—especially when your camera's in those "tight" spaces.

Work Lights

Chances are you don't have professional lighting equipment at your disposal. No big deal. Encased in bright yellow or bright orange plastic with metal grills over the front, work lights are the poor filmmaker's best friend—bright, durable, and versatile. And they're available at most home improvement stores for less than $50.

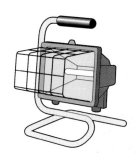

Scoops

Dirt cheap and available at any neighborhood hardware store, "scoops" are aluminum bowl-shaped fixtures with a clamp for attaching to just about anything. They may not be pretty, but they're dirt cheap and they provide plenty of light.

Dolly

A platform for moving the camera smoothly across a flat surface. There are dozens of Web sites with instructions for building your own skateboard dolly easily and inexpensively. For the pornographer who desires a more Hollywood look, this tool is indispensable.

C-Light

For truly professional pornographic close-ups, use a C-light—that is, a small light attached to the end of a pole (for your purposes, a flashlight duct-taped to a broomstick will do the trick). When the camera goes in for a close-up, a crew member thrusts the C-light into the heart of the action, making sure there are no shadows getting in the way of the viewer's good time. What's the "C" stand for? Take your pick.

Baby Wipes

You'll want to have plenty of these handy. Get the scented ones if possible. You'll thank yourself later.

Lube

On a porn set, having water-based lubricant is just as important as having water-based life forms.

Booze

Chances are your talent's going to need a little loosening up. Having a few stiff ones makes it easier to have a few stiff ones.

How to Title Your Masterpiece

Everyone knows a porno is only as good as its title. Here are a few things to keep in mind during the most important phase of production:

1 Don't be lazy. Anyone can slap *Bustin' Nuts in Sluts' Butts* on the side of a video box (it's a helluva film, by the way). But you're better than that. You want a title that does more than state the obvious. You want it to be clever and memorable. You want it to set a mood. For example, something like *Trampire* does it all.

2 Again, parody never fails. You can't argue with the sheer comic brilliance of titles like *Shaving Ryan's Privates* and *Jurassic Pork*. (Seriously, don't argue. You'll lose.) Virtually any movie or TV show will do. *The West Wing* becomes *The Breast Wing*, *The Guest Wing*, *The Best Fling*, or *The West Wang*. The Tom Cruise catalog yields beauties like *Frisky Business*, *Porn on the Fourth of July*, *Missionary: Impossible*, and *The Firm*. See how easy?

3 Go "arty." If all else fails, pick something totally baffling like *Looking for Kansas*. Mainstream filmmakers discovered that "mysterious = genius" a long time ago, and porn was, as usual, right behind them.

☆ the shoot

You've plotted and schemed. You've begged, borrowed, and stolen. Now it's time to bring your porno to life. But even the best concept combined with all the planning in the world means nothing without top-notch "sexecution."

Lighting the Set

And before he did commit the pornography to videotape, the director looked and said, "Let there be light." And he saw the light, and it sucked.

Ninety-nine percent of porn lighting is flat, ugly, and poorly conceived. Now, I'm a pragmatist—I know you can't spend all day trying to create something beautiful when you have seventeen gang bangs to crank out in one afternoon. But there's a solution. I call it my "Unified Theory of Porno Lighting." It goes like this: Make everything *really* dark. Pornos have done "bright" to death. Use shadows. Use flashlights. Cover your actors' naked bodies with glow sticks. Do *anything* to keep your porno from looking . . . well, like a porno. Some other tips:

Find That Box

Most houses aren't equipped to handle a bunch of lights crammed into one electrical outlet. Fuses get blown all the time, so before you start shooting, it's a good idea to track down the circuit box just in case.

Go Soft

People's faces tend to look better in "soft" (indirect) light. When shooting close-ups, try bouncing the light off a piece of white poster board.

Watch and Learn

Steal from the pros. Dig into that DVD collection and pick a few scenes that have a "look" you really like. Then do your best to shamelessly rip off that look with .0003 percent of the original's budget.

Coverage

In the film world, this means shooting lots of different angles to be cut together later. The better you "cover" a scene, the more interesting it'll be to watch. There are five basic elements a director should know:

Blocking a Scene

Essentially, this means creating a plan for how and when the actors move. It's important that your actors repeat the same movements in every take, otherwise you'll find yourself struggling to make cuts match up in editing.

The "Master" Shot

A wide shot that encompasses all of the action, all of the time. Directors usually begin by shooting the master and letting the scene run from beginning to end. (Hint: If you get screwed in editing, the master shot is your "bail out"—there to save you when there's nothing else to cut to.)

The Medium Shot

Comes next. This shot trims the surrounding scenery away and focuses on the people. If your characters have physical contact (and let's hope so, since this is a porno), you'll see most of it in the medium shot.

Close-Ups

Self-explanatory. Each actor gets a close-up. It's your job as the director to make sure their acting is at its least "pornlike" during these takes.

Extreme Close-Ups

These can only be found in pornographic movies. Remember, it isn't sexy unless we can see individual hairs. Of course, if you *have* hairs down there, you're breaking a sacred rule of porn (see page 168)!

Working with Talent

Chances are, that "talent" is your wife, girlfriend, or, in some parts of the world, your sister. But that doesn't mean she should be treated like anything less than porn royalty. Remember, she's sacrificing her last shred of dignity for your stupid stroke flick. These tricks of the trade will help her (and you) through a long day's shooting:

Booze

The lawyers have insisted that I preface with the following: "This book, its author, and publisher in no way advocate the use of alcohol by minors." That said, a few cocktails can go a long way toward easing the inhibitions of both of you.

Mood Music

Set the mood by cranking up some "sex-friendly" tunes. You can't go wrong with

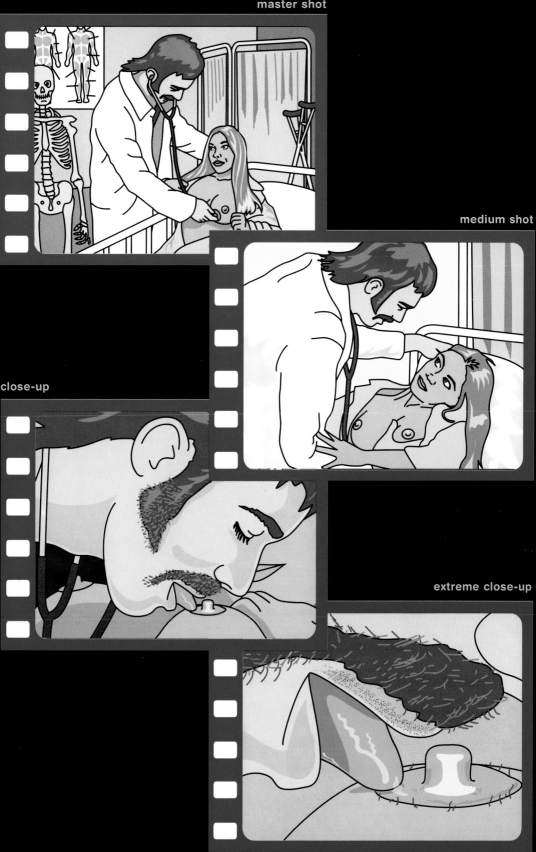

master shot

medium shot

close-up

extreme close-up

strip club staples like Mötley Crüe, Nine Inch Nails, and Jay-Z. However, one note of anything by Bette Midler can bring your porn shoot to a screeching halt.

Romance

Listen, guys, I know it's not easy, but if there was ever a time to step up to the cuddle plate—this is it. Be complimentary and reassuring. Tell her how beautiful she looks, how much you love her, and let her know that she's in control (even if she has been sipping liquor all afternoon). And would it *kill* you to bring her flowers once in a while?

Terms Every Porn Director Should Know

"Cumaway, The": The cutaway shot of a man's face as he cums. After the actual pop shot, it's the most important thing you'll film all day. (Hint: In editing, cut to his "oh yeah" face near the end of the ejaculation. Then cut back to ejaculation from the beginning. Presto! You've just doubled the size of his load!)

"Mish": Short for "missionary," as in, "Let's start with mish, then move to doggy, then BJ, and then we'll break for dinner."

"Piston Shot" (a.k.a. "Meat Shot"): An extreme close-up of penetration—the bread and butter of porn camera angles.

"RC" (a.k.a. "Reverse Cowgirl"): An extremely popular porn-sition because of its camera-friendliness. The woman sits on top of the man facing away from him. Frequently he'll be sitting in a chair, and she'll place her feet on his thighs for support.

"Two-Way": Not what you think. It actually refers to the method of using two cameras to shoot the sex simultaneously. The "hard" camera is for regular full-on porn viewers and the "soft" camera is for cable and hotel room viewers. (The soft camera avoids showing any actual penetration.) Later, two versions of the movie are cut—one for each market.

☆ post-production to premiere

That's a wrap. You did it. You actually convinced people to help you make a porno. Now, all that stands between you and greatness is some good old-fashioned ass-meets-chair time. Editing is the most important part of the porno-making process. How a film is put together can often determine whether it becomes a classic or a disaster. With so much riding on every splice, you'll need all the help you can get.

Cutting It Together

Gone are the days of hooking two VCRs together. There are plenty of affordable editing programs out there (many under $100), assuming your computer has what it takes to run them. Most of the Macs and PCs on the market come with everything you need to get started:

★ A **FireWire port** (or IEEE 1394 port to all you geeks out there) to connect your camera and computer.

★ A **DVD/RW drive** to burn your masterpiece.

★ A **fast video card and processor.**

Music

As long as your porno is for private use only, you can use any music you damn well please. However, if you're planning on posting it to the Web or selling it out of your van in stadium parking lots, you can only use music you have the rights to—meaning a signed agreement with the copyright holder (usually the artist). So, fire up the typewriter and get cracking on that letter to Moby. For more info, try musicforyourfilm.com.

Graphics and Effects

Keep it simple, stud. Nothing says "amateur" like a bunch of crazy star-shaped wipes between every shot. Cuts, fades, and dissolves are all you'll need. As for graphics, save them for the end. Nobody wants to sit through three minutes of: Executive Producer (Your Name Here), Produced by (Your Name Here), Written by (Your Name Here), and Directed by (Your Name Here). They know you did it all by yourself. Just get to the humping already.

Need More Help?

Look to the following sources for advice, inspiration, and support.

★ **Adultfilmmaking.com:** Dedicated to teaching people how to make their own pornos safely, legally, and profitably. Features state-by-state legal advice, tips on finding performers, and budgeting strategies.

★ **Atmospheric-entertainment.com:** A group of young, enthusiastic filmmakers in Minneapolis. The perfect example of how much you can do with limited resources. If this doesn't inspire you to be ambitious, nothing will.

★ **Filmmaking.com:** Everything the independent pornographer could ever need, all under one roof. Instructional articles, equipment advice, and more tutorials than you could shake a $20 tripod at.

★ **Group101films.com:** A Los Angeles–based filmmaking "collective" that challenges its members to complete a short film every thirty days. Relax, you don't have to live in Los Angeles to participate. There are chapters in Charlotte, Chicago, Copenhagen, Dallas, Denver, Karachi, Las Vegas, London, Long Island, Orlando, Phoenix, New York City, San Francisco, and Winnipeg.

★ **Homemade Porn Movie Kit:** Don't feel like going through all this trouble? A company called Topco sells a "Do-It-Yourself Adult Movie Kit." It comes complete with a slate (that chalkboard thingy they use in Hollywood movies), advice for shooting your scene, massage oil, a vibrator, and even some good old-fashioned porn music to set the mood. It'll set you back a reasonable $19.99, although I wouldn't use the character names they suggest—"Spike" and "Spice." Sounds like a cooking show for dogs.

Sharing Your Work

If by some miracle you turn out to be the Spielberg of porn, don't let that masterpiece sit on the bookshelf collecting dust. Proceed directly to one of the following and collect the praise you so richly deserve.

Porn Film Festivals

Yes, they exist. Yes, people take them seriously. Even *before* the inspirational book in your hands was published, amateur pornographers existed in numbers that warranted film festivals on more than one continent.

★ **Hollywood Adult Film Festival (July):** A panel of industry experts judges amateur films and hands out awards for best director, actor, and actress.

★ **Barcelona International Erotic Film Festival (October):** Accepts amateur submissions up to thirty minutes in length and hands out cash prizes.

★ **SinCine NYC Erotic Film Fest (October):** "Skin not necessary, but it is appreciated." Prizes and parties for a whole month near the Chelsea Market.

Web Sites

There's no shortage of pay sites featuring porn amateurs, but precious few are interested in creativity. While you're not likely to find too much hard-core action at these Web addresses, you *will* find plenty of work by other filmmaking novices.

★ **Ifilm.com:** Arguably the best place for amateur filmmakers to showcase their work online. Features an "uncensored" area that's tailor-made for amateur erotica (I say "erotica" because there are limits to what they'll show—best to check out the site first). If your film is up to muster, Ifilm has been known to market DVD compilations, too.

★ **Atomfilms.com:** Like Ifilm, there's a limit to what they'll show. However, it's the perfect target for porn parodies and "mockumentaries."

★ **The Author:** Despite my incredibly busy schedule (i.e., *Full House* marathon on TV Land), I'm always willing to take a look at the work of an aspiring pornographer. If you have a homemade porno, feel free to e-mail it to pornbook@sbcglobal.net. If I don't get back to you for a while, it means I'm *really* enjoying your work.

Sneaking *any* of these porn-sitions into your film may prove challenging, but when you see those tears of joy and amazement in the audiences' eyes, it'll all be worth it.

Porn-sitions

Blumpkin, The: A man receives oral pleasure while sitting on the toilet doing his dirty business.

Bronco, The: When situated behind his partner, the man grabs on tight just before climaxing and yells out another woman's name. He then holds on for dear life while she tries to buck him off.

Dog in a Bathtub: The act of trying to insert testicles in the anus. Keeping a dog in a bathtub is equally challenging.

Gaylord Perry: The name of this famed baseball pitcher is ceremoniously shouted when a depth of two or more knuckles is achieved in a partner's backside. (Perry was one of the few pitchers known for throwing a knuckleball.)

Glass Bottom Boat: An oldie but goodie. Taking care to keep breathing passages open, the partner's face is covered with plastic wrap, and then coated with the bodily waste of choice.

Pirate Maker, The: A man repeatedly pokes his partner in the eye with his erection.

Rear Admiral, The: With both participants standing, the man proudly places his hands on his hips and "steers" his partner around the room.

Screwnicorn, The: Wearing a strap-on dildo on her head, a woman penetrates her partner like a mythical beast.

Tupperware Party: Filling all three of a woman's orifices at the same time.

Zombie Mask, The: The fine art of covering a partner's eyes with ejaculate, thus causing him or her to fumble around the room like the undead.

the screw-nicorn

James Avalon (not his real name) was never destined for porn. In fact, James the teenager probably would've gagged at the thought of working in "filth." He grew up an Oregon Mormon—a double dose of straight and narrow if ever there was one. His love of film emerged at Brigham Young University (itself no stranger to the straight and narrow). Indeed, it looked as if James was on a collision course with a life of white picket fences and pension plans . . . until something extraordinary happened.

He met some hippies.

How they got anywhere near the BYU campus remains a mystery, but nevertheless, James's new friends introduced him to a different world—a world of magic mushrooms, skinny-dipping, and strobe lights. The next chapter almost writes itself: He fell for a flower girl and followed her to California. It didn't work out, so he hung around Los Angeles, even sleeping in his car for a while. A buddy just happened to work for a porno magazine, and James got a job as an assistant editor. It was the middle of the classic era, and soon he was getting steady jobs as a set photographer. That led to stints as a porn reviewer, an award-winning editor (for legendary porn director Greg Dark), and, finally, an AVN award-winning director in his own right. He's helmed dozens of scenes and big-budget porn features like *Les Vampyres*—a film that earned him an AVN award (the industry's top honor) for Best Director in 2001. The X-Rated Critics Organization (XRCO) inducted him into its hall of fame in 2004, the same year that Avalon founded his own production company, Intimate Media.

I sat down to chat with Avalon on several occasions. My goal? Obtain some expert tips to supplement "The Porn Director's Handbook." His goal? Teach me how to surf (there are surfboards in almost every room of Avalon's beachfront home). One of us succeeded.

Avalon's Three Commandments

No matter what part of the porn-making process we were talking about, I noticed that Avalon kept returning to three basic themes. In honor of his religious upbringing, I've organized them into commandments.

❶ Thou Shalt Compromise

Filmmaking is an exercise in problem solving. Yes, things will go wrong. No, you'll never have enough time or money to get what you want. As a director, your job is to roll with the punches—to make the best out of what's available.

❷ Honor Thy Editor

Even if that editor is *you*. Since most pornos don't have the benefit of shot-by-shot storyboards, it's hard to know what you'll end up needing in the cutting room. The more footage you shoot, the easier it will be to put together a coherent, visually interesting scene.

❸ Thou Shalt Not Steal

Don't just copy someone else's style—create your own (just because you're making a porno doesn't mean it has to look like one). Be experimental. Be ambitious. After all, nobody has to see it if it sucks. Well, except you.

The Story

"If it ain't on the page, it ain't on the stage." An old show business adage that sums up the importance of having a plan—whether it's a detailed script or a one-sentence idea. What should your porno be about? Avalon has a few suggestions:

Look to the Past

You can't go wrong updating a story from classic literature. Imagine the possibilities of porno-fying a Jane Austen, Ernest Hemingway, William Shakespeare, or Mark Twain story. *The Old Man and the Semen*? Brilliant! *The Adventures of Fuckleberry Finn*? Genius!

Create Obstacles

Whatever the story, don't let your stud score without working for it. The deeper the ditch you put him in (he can't find his penis; he's been reincarnated as a cucumber), the bigger the payoff when he finally gets some.

Introduce a Stranger

If you're stuck for ideas, a knock at the door always does the trick, though try to avoid the old pizza boy cop-out. Why not make a Jehovah's Witness porno? (That was a rhetorical question, smart ass.)

Elements of Style

Most porn-fessionals skip this step, but Avalon's made a career out of giving his films a "look." Learning how to create those sexy visuals took years of trial and error, so, naturally, I asked him to condense all that experience into a pair of easy-to-digest bullet points.

Use Deep, Dark Colors

Deep, dark reds, oranges, and blues heighten sexuality, while bright colors tend to distract from the mood. This applies to walls, bedsheets, makeup, props, and light-ing. Electric-green duvet cover? Bad idea.

Mix It Up

Try using different shooting styles and methods in the same film. Used together, grainy black and white and crisp color can create a "music video" feel that keeps those fingers off the fast-forward button.

The Shoot

When the big day arrives, you probably won't have any idea what the hell you're doing (I mean, you're currently enrolled in a fifteen-minute film school). But that doesn't mean anyone needs to be the wiser. Consider this James Avalon's clip-and-carry cheat sheet.

go easy on the spackle

Hair and Makeup

Go easy on the spackle (after all, these are porn actresses—we wouldn't want them to look like hookers). A little bit of base and eyeliner is all you need. Augment your starlet's natural features—don't repaint her entire face. As for the hair? Forget the stuff on top—it's that *other* hair we're concerned with. Whether your talent is male or female, don't let them reach for the razor. Avalon assures me that waxed looks a *lot* better on camera.

Lighting

Home video cameras are designed to shoot without the aid of big, professional lights, but that doesn't mean you can simply flip on the fluorescents and go (actually, fluo-rescent light is just about the *worst* thing you can shoot in). Lighting should be "prac-tical" (coming from something on-screen, like a desk lamp) or "motivated" (made to look like it's coming from a believable source, like a window). If your scene is indoors, put 150-watt bulbs in all the light fixtures (don't burn the place down) and have some white poster board handy. It's great for bouncing light into those "hard to reach" spots.

Camera

Give the scene an opening shot that creates interest. Open on something that will grab the audience's attention, like a close-up of a pony wearing lingerie (the pony's my suggestion, not Avalon's. Still, it's hot, right?). Try to stay off the tripod as much as possible—the more camera movement, the more you'll keep your audience interested. Try to frame creatively, so you see sex and facial expressions in the same shot.

Working with Talent

Real-life feelings are internal, but porn isn't real life—so they need to be vocalized for the camera. In Avalon's experience, about 70 percent of performers need prodding to be vocal, so don't be shy about reminding them. Feed them word-for-word "oh, yeahs" if necessary. If you run into the porn director's nightmare—a man with wood problems—shoot everything else, and then go in for a close-up with a "stunt dick." When working with women, be encouraging—don't make them self-conscious. Make an ice-breaking joke (one of Avalon's favorite bits is asking, "So, should we just get the double anal out of the way first?").

Editing

If you make it through your shoot in one piece, there's still the small matter of putting it all together into something sexy and entertaining. Editing can make a good film great—but it can also make a great film horrible. Here are some final tips from Dean James Avalon to accompany your fifteen-minute film school diploma. Good luck!

Music

"It's better to have no music than bad music" (for this reason, most of Avalon's films are composed to order). Music is the key to emotion. If you use fast, cheap, and repetitive music, it could kill the scene. Use tracks that enhance the mood you're trying to create (tension, excitement) without distracting the audience from what's happening on-screen.

Helping a Bad Scene

If your scene just isn't "hot enough," call your leading lady back and record a few minutes of her moaning with delight. Mix this in with the final cut to create more eroticism than there actually was.

7

extra
features

Well, looks like the ol' Erection Express has just about reached the end
of the tracks. If I may say so, you've come a hell-uva long way. Two hundred pages ago, you were hardly worth the scar tissue on a bad boob
job. Now you're ready to face even the grimiest adult bookstore with
confidence. I'm proud of you, and I hope the world of pornos is a little
less frightening. After all, if I can save just one person from spontaneously combusting the next time a nipple appears on TV, well, then my
quest hasn't been in vain. I'd like to leave you with a few more tools to
stuff in that shiny new porno toolbox of yours—a few quotes, a few defi-
nitions, and a few more places to expand your dirty horizons. Now get
out there and make me proud. And remember: Somewhere there's a
Japanese businessman enjoying what you're afraid to try.

Every industry has its own lingo, and porn is no exception. Being fluent in the language of dirty movies is essential when navigating an adult bookstore, describing your kinks to a sex partner, or searching the Internet for new and exciting fetishes. It'll also make you the coolest eighth-grader in your entire school.

69: Named for the shape formed by their bodies, 69 occurs when partners give each other simultaneous oral pleasure. It's also the maximum combined age of couples who can pull it off without looking completely ridiculous.

Analingus: The act of licking the anus or inserting one's tongue into the anus. Also known as RIMMING.

Autoerotic Asphyxiation: The dangerous act of partially strangling oneself during sex or masturbation, based on the belief that a lack of oxygen to the brain heightens orgasm. (Warning: *This can kill you.* Don't try it, period. If you want to experience an orgasm with a lack of oxygen, masturbate in Denver.)

Auto-Fellatio: The act of sucking one's own penis; reserved for men who've been exceptionally blessed.

Bareback: Sex without a condom.

Barely Legal: In porn, any woman who's between the ages of eighteen and twenty-eight isn't legal—she's *barely* legal.

Beef Curtains: The rather unfortunate nickname given to a woman's labia. Don't ask what "creamed chipped beef on toast" is.

Bisexual: Anyone who desires sex with both genders. In the world of porn, this can also mean "woman."

BJ: An abbreviation of "blowjob." Also known as FELLATIO and HEAD.

Blind Man: An uncircumcised penis.

Body Inflation: A fetish for grossly exaggerated body parts—breasts, thighs, ears, you name it. It can be depicted through drawings or simulated with skintight latex suits. (The suits are connected to air or helium tanks and inflated, turning the wearer into a walking balloon.)

barely
legal

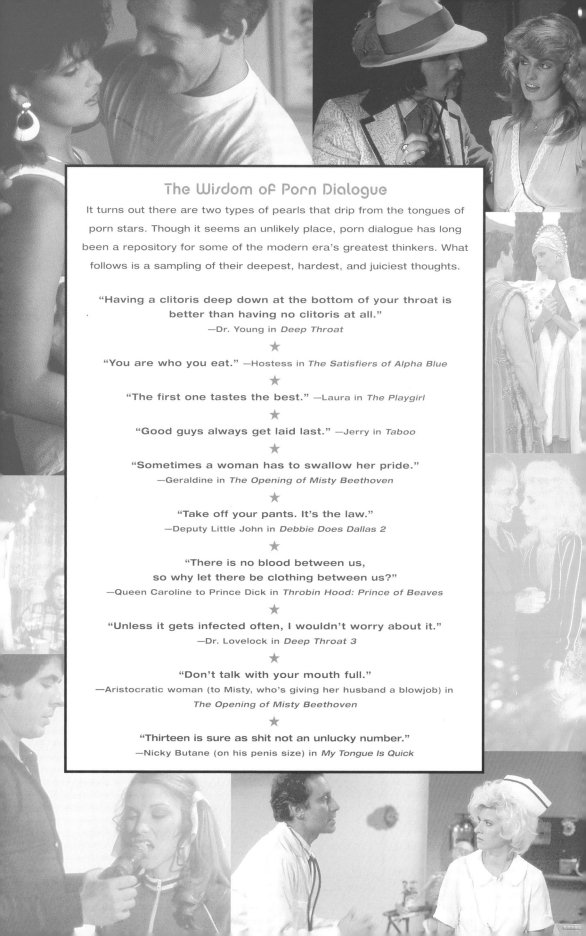

The Wisdom of Porn Dialogue

It turns out there are two types of pearls that drip from the tongues of porn stars. Though it seems an unlikely place, porn dialogue has long been a repository for some of the modern era's greatest thinkers. What follows is a sampling of their deepest, hardest, and juiciest thoughts.

"Having a clitoris deep down at the bottom of your throat is better than having no clitoris at all."
—Dr. Young in *Deep Throat*

★

"You are who you eat." —Hostess in *The Satisfiers of Alpha Blue*

★

"The first one tastes the best." —Laura in *The Playgirl*

★

"Good guys always get laid last." —Jerry in *Taboo*

★

"Sometimes a woman has to swallow her pride."
—Geraldine in *The Opening of Misty Beethoven*

★

"Take off your pants. It's the law."
—Deputy Little John in *Debbie Does Dallas 2*

★

**"There is no blood between us,
so why let there be clothing between us?"**
—Queen Caroline to Prince Dick in *Throbin Hood: Prince of Beaves*

★

"Unless it gets infected often, I wouldn't worry about it."
—Dr. Lovelock in *Deep Throat 3*

★

"Don't talk with your mouth full."
—Aristocratic woman (to Misty, who's giving her husband a blowjob) in
The Opening of Misty Beethoven

★

"Thirteen is sure as shit not an unlucky number."
—Nicky Butane (on his penis size) in *My Tongue Is Quick*

cock

Bottom: In the world of BDSM, this is the name given to the more submissive sexual partner. A "Power Bottom" is a gay man who enjoys being on the receiving end of a good hammering.

Bubble Gum: An excessive amount of pink skin around a woman's labia.

C.B.T.: "Cock and ball torture." This isn't a fetish for the faint of heart. During a typical session, the testicles and penis are subjected to mind-numbing acts of aggression. They're nailed to boards, crushed in vices, stomped with stilettos, and worse.

Cock: The penis. Also known as BOLOGNA PONY, CHUB,

DICK, DONG, HOSE, JEROME'S CANE, JOHN THOMAS, JOHNSON, JUNK, MAIN VEIN, ONE-EYED JACK, PECKER, PETER, PRICK, PUD, ROD, SALAMI, SAUSAGE, SCHLONG, SKIN FLUTE, SPELUNKER, TOOL, TROUSER SNAKE, TUBE STEAK, WANG, WIENER, and WILLY.

Cock Ring: Band (usually metal or rubber) that serves a dual sexual purpose—maintaining an erection and heightening the pleasure of its recipient.

Corsetting: A fetish for modifying the body or restricting oxygen intake with dangerously tight corsets.

Creampie: A vagina after an internal ejaculation.

Crewkake: When a female porn star decides to reward the crew for a hard day's work by letting them masturbate onto her. Adapted from the Japanese term "bukkake" (see page 130).

Cum: Semen. Also known as APHRODITE'S TOOTHPASTE, BABY BATTER, BALL BUTTER, COCK VOMIT, EXHIBIT "A," GENTLEMAN'S RELISH, JIZZ, LOAD, MAN MAYO, MANTHRAX, NUT NECTAR, PECKER SNOT, PENIS PASTE, SEED, SPOOGE, SPUNK, TESTICLE TAPIOCA, THE BOARDING PARTY, THE KIDS, THE SWIM TEAM, WAD, WHITE GOLD, and YUCK.

D.A.T.Y.: "Dining at the 'Y.'" Named for the shape of a woman's body when her legs are spread out, it refers to the act of oral pleasure.

Docking: Inserting the penis into the foreskin of another man's penis. Warning: Make sure you have a good seal or you're likely to get blown out into space!

Doggie Style: A woman is penetrated from behind while she braces herself on all fours.

D.P.: "Double penetration." Specifically, when a woman is vaginally and anally penetrated at the same time.

D.V.D.A.: "Double Vaginal, Double Anal." The seemingly unattainable feat of stuffing four penises in one woman (and still leaving her free to sing a Gershwin tune). It's also the name of a band formed by *South Park* creators Trey Parker and Matt Stone.

Edge Play: Sex that can lead to serious injury or death.

Felching: Removing ejaculate from a partner's anus with a straw. (Hey, don't blame me. I don't make this stuff up.)

Filling the Pool: Ejaculating in the belly button. Also known as FIXING A POTHOLE, SPACKLING, and STOMPING A DIVOT.

F.I.P.: "Fake Internal Pop" shot. While inside his partner, a man fakes an orgasm—convulsing and grunting for the camera (used in the "soft-core" cable versions of pornos).

Fisting: The act of inserting a hand, foot, arm, leg, or—in rare cases—*head* into the vagina or anus.

Fluffer: A woman responsible for keeping a male porn star erect between shots. Despite the endless supply of jokes, real fluffers are extremely rare, especially since the advent of those little blue pills. Men are second-class citizens in the porn world. They're hired for their ability to get and stay hard at will. Porno etiquette dictates that the female costar "help him out" before the scene.

fisting

Garfunkling: Going down on a white woman whose pubic hair is especially bushy.

Glory Hole: Usually found in bathroom stalls, these are holes that men stick their penises through to be pleasured by a mystery man or woman on the other side.

Golden Shower: The act of urinating on a partner during sex.

Gunboats: Breasts with erect nipples.

Huffing: Performing oral sex on a man.

Hunting Bin Laden: Flooding one of your partner's orifices with liquid, either through an enema or by urinating into them.

Looner: The common term for someone with a balloon fetish. Some looners are "poppers"—those who get off on the suspense of a balloon being squeezed or inflated to the breaking point. "Nonpoppers" usually prefer to play with the balloons during sex, or to have sex with the balloon itself.

Macrofile: A man who fantasizes about gigantic women—we're talking Godzilla-sized women. They often get off on the thought of being stomped on (like the Japanese "foot-crush" craze) or gobbled up.

M.I.L.F.: "Mother I'd like to fuck." An attractive older woman.

Money Shot: A shot capturing the all-important ejaculation. Also known as CUM SHOT and POP SHOT.

huffing

Oculolinctus: According to Brenda Love's *Encyclopedia of Unusual Sex Practices*, this is the act of sexually licking an eyeball.

Pussy: The vagina. Also known as BEARDED CLAM, BOX, COCK TUB, COOTER, GARAGE, GASH, HAIR PIE, HONEYPOT, HOO-HA, LOVE GLOVE, MEAT SLIPPER, MICHAEL CORLEONE'S SAFEHOUSE, MOOSE KNUCKLE, MUFF, PINK TACO, POONTANG, SNATCH, THE FRONT DOOR, TWAT, and VERTICAL SMILE.

Raincoater: A man who frequents adult bookstores, and who generally has a large personal collection of smut. Named for the attire worn by most men in porn theaters.

Roman Shower: The act of intentionally vomiting on your partner. Named for the trips to the vomitorium that usually followed ancient Rome's wild parties.

Running a Red Light: Having sex with a woman during her period.

San Fernando Shower: Cleaning oneself with baby wipes after a sex scene. Named for the San Fernando Valley, the heart of America's porn industry.

Skiing: When a woman is situated between two men giving them both hand jobs. (If you need a definition for "hand job," put this book down and go meet some people.)

Snore, The: Another way of saying "missionary position." Also known as 1.0 and MISH.

Suitcase Pimp: Husbands or boyfriends of porn stars. The stereotypical suitcase pimp is a controlling (and sometimes abusive) leech who hangs out on sets all day trying to seem important.

Tadpole: A younger man who sleeps with substantially older women.

Tush Pizza: The unsightly pimples that often cover a porn starlet's rear end.

Weatherproofing: Pulling out and ejaculating between the butt cheeks.

Woodsman: A male porn star. Also known as COCK-SMITH and MEAT PUPPET.

Think You Might Have a Porn Problem?

Most Vegas casinos display pamphlets for Gambler's Anonymous. Therefore, I feel compelled to provide the following public service. If your habit is spiraling out of control, go to one of these Web sites.

★ **No-porn.com:** Includes a test designed to tell you if you need help or not. (I got an "F." What's that mean?)

★ **Firesofdarkness.com:** Offers a step-by-step guide to defeating your porn addiction, including links to outside resources and a section with the unfortunate title "Hope for the hurting wife."

★ **Porn-free.org:** Claims that "possibly millions" of people become porn addicts every day. Wait a second—let's do some math. Assuming that one million people become addicted to porn daily, then every man, woman, and child on earth would be hooked in a little over sixteen years.

porn resources

For those of you interested in furthering your porn educations, graduate degrees are only a few mouse clicks away.

Adameve.com: This North Carolina–based company is the Web's biggest retailer of sex toys and accessories. And to my knowledge, it's the only place you can get a customer's dildo review in English *and* Spanish.

Adamfilmworld.com: The site isn't much to speak of, but it is the easiest way to subscribe to the industry's longest-running trade magazine. Every year *AFW* puts out a comprehensive directory of films and performers. It's considered a "must-own" item by all self-respecting smut peddlers.

Aim-med.org: The home of the Adult Industry Medical Health Care Foundation—Dr. Sharon Mitchell's nonprofit organization dedicated to the "physical and emotional needs" of porn workers.

Avn.com: Official site of the industry's biggest trade publication. News items updated around the clock, in-depth articles, resources, reviews, top-rental and sales charts, events calendars, and a comprehensive industry directory. The best adult information site on the Web.

Avninsider.com: Another site from the industry giant, but worth mentioning on its own. This one features editorials written by the biggest people in porn—Jenna Jameson, "The Decadent Bridgette" and Skeeter Kerkove, and Dave Cummings, "the oldest active porn star in the business." Much more of a behind-the-scenes slant.

Creampie.com: Someone's actually taken the time to create a searchable database of porn movies that feature internal money shots. The site also includes some of the most ridiculously gigantic close-ups of vaginas ever committed to film.

Erosblog.com: A great place for porn aficionados to congregate and share their love of filth. Amusing posts, free pictures, and links to some of the weirdest things you'll ever see.

Freddyandeddy.com: A site aimed at the couple who likes to enjoy their porn together. Movie suggestions, product reviews, sales, and articles like "How to Pick a Sex Toy."

Furnitureporn.com: Hot chair-on-chair action, sofa bondage, and "hot gay teen lawn chair" sex. You won't see any human beings going at it. Just furniture. Slutty, slutty furniture.

Goodvibes.com: Female-owned (a growing trend in the world of smut), Good Vibrations has been "promoting sexual health and pleasure" since 1977. The site takes a more intellectual approach to smut. There's tons of erotica for sale, tips for improving the quality of your sex life, and a (fascinating) antique vibrator museum. You have to see it to believe it.

Hardcoregossip.com: Delivers what it promises, as well as regular news items and interviews with your favorite adult stars. The writing staff's sense of humor makes this a more enjoyable read than most adult news sites.

Iafd.com: The Internet adult film database covers nearly fifty-thousand movies and forty-thousand stars and filmmakers. The site includes biographical information for all your favorite porn stars and links to fan-written reviews.

Janesguide.com: Committed to helping Web-goers "cut through the garbage," Jane reviews thousands of porn sites so you don't have to.

Lukeford.com: The closet thing porn has to the *Drudge Report*—opinions, gossip, and exposés. Ford first encountered porn in 1995, and it didn't take him long to become one of the most hated (and feared) people in the industry. It wasn't his conservative slant that got him blackballed, it was his proclivity for posting rumors and breaking "the code"—the unwritten rule that what happens in the industry, stays in the industry. (Ford is no longer affiliated with the site that bears his name, but you can still rifle through his fascinating archives and get up-to-date dirt from its new owners.)

Penisbot.com: A huge collection of adult links organized into easy-to-navigate categories. The vast majority are links to "free" galleries (i.e., a few nude pics accompanied by an offer to sign up).

Purplepassion.com: This fetish retailer is heaven on earth for people who demand more from the bondage experience. An enormous selection of masks, gags, chastity belts, latex gear, spiky objects, whips, clamps, and much, much more. Also features an events calendar and newsletter for the BDSM enthusiast.

Rame.net: Everything a porn lover needs: reviews, FAQs, resources, trade show updates, star bios, industry news, links, and adult classifieds.

Realdoll.com: Want your very own porn star? Since 1996, RealDoll has been using Hollywood special effects techniques and materials to produce the closest thing to a woman that money can buy. Fleshlike silicone, articulated skeletons, and customizable everything (they mean *everything*—you can even choose her fingernail color). Oh, and ladies? They make male dolls, too.

Sinspin.com: A public relations company dedicated to the world of "X," representing big companies and individual porn stars alike.

Stopclownpornnow.org: Finally, an organization that addresses the urgent problem of clowns in pornography. The site relies on donations to "purchase domain names that might be used by clown pornographers in the future," and to maintain a shelter "for clowns trying to get out of the porn industry." Bravo.

Ten Reputable Retailers

All of these sites feature quality product (no pirated copies), customer service, safe billing, and discreet shipping at fair prices:

Adultdvdandtoys.com

Adultdvdempire.com

Adultdvdnow.com

Adultmoviedatabase.com

Amazingdirect.com

Moviesbymail.com

Sexdvd.com

Videoage.com

Wantedlist.com

Xxx-dvd-online.com

☆ porn the whole year round

No matter where in the world you live, there are enough adult-themed activities to keep you busy through winter, spring, summer, and fall!

January

★ **The Adult Entertainment Expo (Las Vegas):** The largest adult trade show in the United States, and the best weekend to be in Vegas, period. Good luck booking a room.

★ **The AVN Awards (Las Vegas):** *Entertainment Weekly* calls them "the Oscars of Adult"—a full-scale gala recognizing the best that porn has to offer.

★ **Just for Grownups (Toronto):** The Canucks need their trade shows, too. This one features everything from furniture to penis pumps.

February

★ **Pantheon of Leather (Chicago):** A three-day celebration of the BDSM lifestyle. The event includes an awards ceremony recognizing the year's most distinguished "leatherfolk."

★ **Nude Valentine's Bungee Jumping (Nanaimo, British Columbia):** Celebrate Valentine's Day by stripping down and leaping from a bridge with your special someone.

March

★ **Texas Latex Party (Houston):** This annual three-day gathering includes a fetish luncheon, a fetish tea party, and, of course, a free commemorative T-shirt.

★ **San Francisco Fetish Ball (San Francisco):** Every year, San Fran's leather-clad fabulous gather for a night of fashion, dancing, performance art, and naked lubricant wrestling.

★ **Portland Kinkfest (Portland, Oregon):** This BDSM expo features workshops ("Anal Pleasure for Everyone"), equipment sales, and a team of "Dungeon Monitors" to keep things under control. Who knew Oregonians were so kinky?

April

★ **Adult Online Europe (Amsterdam, Netherlands):** Webmasters from both sides of the Atlantic gather to network and discuss the latest trends in Internet and mobile phone porn.

★ **Spanking Weekend in the Mountains (near Allentown, Pennsylvania):** Ms. Margaret Davis invites "tops" to bring their "bottoms" to an eighty-five-acre resort for three days of spanking, spanking, and more spanking. And yes, there's a real woodshed on the premises.

May

★ **Annual Masturbation-a-Thon (USA):** Brought to you by the people at *Good Vibrations* magazine, the AMAT raises money for charity just like a walk-a-thon—only the participants never have to leave home! To sponsor a stroker, visit goodvibes.com.

★ **Lifestyles's Desire Resort & Spa (Cancun, Mexico):** The Lifestyles company takes over an idyllic tropical resort for a couples-only weekend of nude beaches, partner-swapping, and outdoor sex. Beats Club Med.

★ **Erotic Expo Brighton (Brighton, England):** With live stage shows, films, magazines, sex toys, and over fifty porn actresses walking the exhibit hall, there's enough to satisfy any porn enthusiast's appetite.

June

★ **FOXE Awards (Los Angeles):** The "Fans of X-Rated Entertainment" bestow their annual awards for porn excellence.

★ **Naked Flight (Miami to Jamaica):** The good people at Castaways Travel have chartered a clothing-optional airliner for those of us who've always dreamed of being naked at 35,000 feet. Visit castawaystravel.com for booking info.

★ **Erotica LA (Los Angeles):** A place for the industry to strut new films, stars, and toys in its own backyard. One of the biggest adult trade shows of the year.

July

★ **Lifestyles West (Las Vegas):** According to its Web site, this convention is a place for couples who are into "sparking the flame of passion and excitement they shared earlier in their relationship." Hmmm . . .

★ **Free Speech Coalition's Night of the Stars (Los Angeles):** This dinner/dance honors adult industry figures who stand up for their First Amendment rights. Or is it "lay down"?

★ **Annual Amtrak Mooning (Laguna Niguel, California):** What started on a dare more than twenty-five years ago has become a time-honored tradition: mooning Amtrak trains. The all-day event now draws over 1,000 people (not including the sold-out trains, which slow down as they pass). Check out moonamtrak.org.

★ **Sexpo (Sydney):** The biggest adult trade show in the land down under. Their motto? "Lighten up, sex is fun!" Indeed.

August

★ **Adult Expo China (Beijing):** Thanks to China's changing climate, the Expo lets citizens explore the worlds of reproductive health and adult entertainment.

★ **Internext Expo (Hollywood, Florida):** If you operate an adult Web site, here's an excuse to get out of your mom's basement and meet some new people.

★ **Gentleman's Club Owners Expo (Las Vegas):** More than three thousand strip club operators descend on Las Vegas. Because if there's one thing Vegas needs, it's more strip club owners.

September

★ *NightMoves* **Adult Entertainment Awards (Clearwater, Florida):** *NightMoves Magazine* presents awards to its readers' favorite films and stars.

★ **Nuit Elastique (Paris):** Beginning in 1998, this monthly rave has grown into the biggest fetish party in Paris—a sea of corsets, rubber, leather, ball-gags, and uniforms. Appropriately, transgender patrons pay five euros more than women at the door, but five less than men.

★ **Budapest Erotic Fair (Budapest):** Live sex shows, autograph booths, body painting, and a "Mrs. Erotica" competition. Not bad for a country that used to take its orders from Moscow.

October

★ **Venus International Trade Show (Berlin):** The year's biggest gathering of European pornographers (the show's organizers encourage them to stay at the Holiday Inn).

★ **Erotic Art Weekend (Los Angeles):** Sponsored by the Tom of Finland Foundation, this annual exhibit aims to bring all forms of erotic art—painting, sculpture, and other media—to the public's attention.

November

★ **Glamourcon (USA):** Love the pinup girls of today and yesteryear? Here's your chance to meet them in person. For more than a decade, Glamourcon has been traveling from city to city with hordes of *Playboy* Playmates and other calendar girls in tow.

★ **Erotica (London):** It's the biggest show of its kind in the world—"the ultimate lifestyle event for any open-minded adult over eighteen." From movies to wigs, sex toys to alternative vacation planners, you'll find anything and everything related to the world of adult entertainment.

December

★ **Have a Very Seymore Christmas (The Privacy of Your Own Home):** Roast your chestnuts with a couple of Seymore Butts holiday classics: *A Christmas Orgy* (1998) and *Merry Fucking Christmas* (1998).

☆300 real porn titles

When it comes to making pornos, it's all in a name. So, I looked under every fleshy fold in the adult world to collect examples of titular excellence. What follows are three hundred of the funniest, cheesiest, weirdest, smartest, and dumbest titles porn has to offer. And yes, all of them come from 100 percent real movies. Now get ready to settle some bets.

20,000 Legs Under the Sea
2069: A Sex Odyssey
28 Gays Later
40 Gays and 40 Dykes

Air Down There, The
All Hands on Dick
Ally McFeel
American Booty
An Officer and a Genitalman
Angela's Asses
Anus the Menace
Apollo 69
Armaget-it-on
Ass Ventura: Smut Detective
Ass Wide Open
Assablanca
Austin Prowler

Ball the President's Men
Barbara's Bush
Bare Wench Project, The
Battlestar Orgasmica
Be Bi Me
Beautiful Grind, A
Beetle's Juice
Ben-Hur Over
Beverly Hills 9021-Ho!
Beverly Hills Cock
Bi-Curious George
Big Trouble in Little Vagina
Bitches of Eat-Wick
Bitches of Madison County, The
Black Cock Down
Bone Alone
Bonfire of the Panties

Booty and the Beast
Bootyguard, The
Bruce Allmeaty
Buffy the Vampire Layer
Butch Lesbian and the Lapdance Kid

Captain Hooker & Peter Porn
Charlie's Anals
Cliff Banger
Clitty Clitty Gang Bangz
Clockwork Orgy, A
Close Encounters of the Sperm Kind
Cockodile Dun-me
Colonel Angus
Cool Bummings
Corporate Assets
Cream On
Crimson Ride
Crouching Penis, Hidden Vagina
Cum and Cummer
Cum Lola Cum
Cum of all Queers, The
Cum to Drink of It
Cumming to America
Cuntry Club
Czech-Mate

Das Booty
Dawson's Crack
Deep End with Some Lotion
Desperately Seeking Semen
Dial M for Missionary
Diddle-her on the Roof
Dildo Baggins: Lord of the Wangs
Dirty Dozen Inches, The
Dog-Style Afternoon

Dominatrix Unloaded, The
Done in 60 Seconds
DP2: The Mighty Phucks
Driving It into Ms. Daisy
Dude, Where's My Dildo?

E-3: The Extra Testicle
Edward Penishands
Ejacula
Emission Possible
Empire Strokes Black, The
Enema of the State
Erectnophobia
Everybody Does Raymond

Fast Times at Deep Crack High
Fatal Erection
Ferris Bueller Gets Off
Few Hard Men, A
Field of Reams
Fill Bill
First of April, The
Fistful of Penis, A
Flesh Gordon
For a Few Inches More
For Your Thighs Only
Fornocopia
Forrest Hump
Frisky Business
Fuckulty, The

Gangbangs of New York
Genital Hospital
Genital's Daughter, The
Gettin' Sticky with It
Ghostlusters
Glad-he-ate-her
Gonad the Barbarian
Good Will Humping
Got Milk? Yes.
Grand Theft Anal
Great Muppet Raper, The
Great Sexpectations
Guess Who Came at Dinner

Hairy Pooter and the Sorcerer's Bone
Halloween: ResERECTION
Hannah Does Her Sisters

Hannibal Lickter
Homo Alone
Honey, I Blew Everybody!
Horney-mooners, The
Horny Python and the Bony Tail
How Stella Got Her Tube Packed
Hung Wankenstein
Hump Up the Volume
Humpback of Nasty Dames, The
Humping from the Back at Notre Dame
Hunt for Head-all-over, The

I Cream on Jeannie
I Know Who You Did Last Summer
In & Out of Beverly Hills
In Diana Jones and the Temple of Poon
Indepoondence Day
Inspect Her Gadget
Intensities in Ten Cities
Intercourse with the Vampire
Invasion of the Booby Snatchers

Jack/Off
Joy Suck Club, The
Juranal Park
Jurassic Pork

King Dong
Kingdom Cum
KSEX 106.9

Lad In, A
Laid in Manhattan
Lap Dances with Wolves
Lawrence of a Labia
League of Their Moan, A
Legally Blown
Legs Wide Open
Little Orphan Anal
Little Red Rubbing Hood
Load Warrior, The
Lock Cock and Two Smoking Bimbos
Loin King, The
Long Ranger, The
Lord of the Cock Rings
Lord of the G-strings
Lord of the Rims
Lust of the Mohicans

Lust Picture Show, The

Maddam's Family, The
Mad Jack: Beyond Thunderbone
Majesdick, The
Malcolm XXX
Mating for Guffman
Meat Joe Black
Meat Pushin' in the Seat Cushion
Meat the Parents
Men in Back
Merry Fucking Christmas
Midsummer Night's Cream, A
Mighty Joe Hung
Miracle on 69th Street
Missionary Position Impossible
Murphy's Brown
Mutiny on the Booty
My Big Fat Greek Cock

Nads-u-ate, The
Naked Bun, The
Night of the Giving Head
No Holes Barred
Nurse Wetty
NYDP Blue
NYPD Goo

Object of My Erection, The
Oh Brother, Who Fuck Thou?
Oh Cum on Ye Faces
Oh She's Eleven
Oklahomo!
On Golden Blonde
One Spewed Over the Cuckoo's Nest
Ozporns, The

Penis Runs Through It, A
Phallus in Wonderland
Picnic at Hanging Cock
Piledriving Miss Daisy
Pimped by an Angel
Playmate of the Apes
Pocahotass
Poke-'em All: The Movie
Politically Erect
Poltergash
Poonies, The

Porn on the Fourth of July
Pornochio
Pourne Identity, The
ProfessiANALS, The
Puck: A Midsummer Night's Debauchery
Pulp Friction

Queer and Present Danger
Quick and the Hard, The

Rambone
Rawshank Redemption
Rear and Pleasant Danger, A
Rebel Without a Condom
Regarding Hiney
Remember the Tight'uns
Reproducers, The
Rodfather, The
Romancing the Bone
Romeo in Juliet
Rosemary's Booby

Saturday Night Beaver
Schindler's Fist
Schindler's Lust
School of Hard Cocks
Screw the Right Thing
Screwman Show, The
Scrotal Recall
Sex Trek: The Next Penetration
Sexcalibur
Sexorcist, The
Sgt. Pecker's Lonely Hearts Club Gangbang
Shake My Spear, I'm in Love
Shavers of the Lost Ass
Shaving Ryan's Privates
Sheepless in Montana
Six Degrees of Penetration
Sixth Inch, The
Sleazy Rider
Sleeping with Seattle
Sling Babes
Slutty Professor, The
Snatch Adams
Snatch Me If You Can
Snoopy Cum Home
Snow White and the Seven Inches

So I Married a Porn Star
Sodomania
Sopornos, The
Sorest Rump
South Pork
Sperminator, The
Sperms of Endearment
Splatman
Splendor in the Ass
Star Whores: The Empire Likes Back
Swallow Hal
Swinging in the Rain

Tailiens
Tale of Two Titties, A
Talented Mr. Lickme, The
Tales from the Clit
Texas Dildo Masquerade, The
There's Something in and out of Mary
Three Men and Some Gravy
Three Men on a Lady
Throbin Hood: Prince of Beaves
Tight Club
Till Sex Do Us Part
Tits a Wonderful Life
Titty Slickers
To Drill a Mockingbird
To Uranus & Back
Too Clothed for Comfort
Toothless People
Touchables, The
Touched by an Uncle
Trampire
Turner and Cooch
Twin Cheeks
Two Lays in the Valley

Varsity Blows

Wet Dreams May Come
Wetness for the Prosecution
What's Eating Gilbert's Grapes?
When Harry Ate Sally
Where the Boy's Aren't
White Men Can't Hump
White Stuff, The
Who Reamed Roger Rabbit?

Whole Nine Inches, The
Whore of the Worlds
Willy Wanker and the Fudge Packing Factory
Witness for the Penetration
Womb Raider

XXX Files, The
XXX-Men

Yank My Doodle, It's a Dandy
Yeastmaster, The
Yo Quiero Taco Smell
Young and the Breastless, The
You've Got Tail

☆ photo credits

The posters on pages 40, 49, 55, 65, and 123 appear courtesy of The X-Rated Collection.
Page 12: Library of Congress (Cornelius); Library of Congress (Three Women); The Vintage
Erotica Foundation (Background). Page 13: Encyclozine (Barrison Sisters); Library of
Congress (Muybridge). Page 14: The Vintage Erotica Foundation. Page 15: Library of
Congress (The Kiss, Thomas Edison); © Science and Society Picture Library (Nickelodeon).
Page 16: Library of Congress (Supreme Court); National Archives (Background). Page 17: ©
Science and Society Picture Library. Page 18: The Vintage Erotica Foundation. Page 19:
Everett Collection. Page 20: Library of Congress (Hitler); © Elektrafilm A. S. (Extase). Page 21:
Everett Collection (Hays); The Vintage Erotica Foundation (Woman). Page 22: © 20th Century
Fox (Bananas); © United Artists (Jane Russell). Page 23: Library of Congress (Hoover). Page
24: National Archives. Page 26: Photo by Hulton Archive/Getty Images. Page 27: © Science
and Society Picture Library (VCR); © Bettman/CORBIS (marquee). Page 28: Photo By Getty
Images. Page 29: Everett Collection. Page 30: © Evil Angel (Buttman), © Private
(Background). Page 31: Strand Releasing/Everett Collection (Annabel), © VCA (Misty). Page
32: Library of Congress (Aretino); The Vintage Erotica Foundation (Small Waist); The Vintage
Erotica Foundation (Reclining). Page 33: Everett Collection (Stern); © The Cover Story/COR-
BIS (Virtual Reality). Page 34: © Private. Page 35: Miramax/Everett Collection. Page 39: ©
VCA. Page 48: © VCA. Page 50: Everett Collection. Page 54: © Bettmann/CORBIS (still).
Page 57: © Video-X-Pix. Page 58: New Line Cinema/Everett Collection. Page 59: USA
Films/Everett Collection. Page 72: © Video-X-Pix. Page 75: © Digital Playground. Page 77: ©
VCA. Pages 77-78: © Private. Page 80: © Digital Playground (Workers). Page 88: © VCX.
Page 90: © VCX (Cousteau, Inset). Page 91: Courtesy of Kay Taylor Parker. Pages 92–93: ©
VCA. Page 94: © VCX (Wine Glass). Page 95: © VCA. Pages 96–97: © VCA. Page 98: © VCA.
Page 99: © VCX. Page 101: © VCA. Page 102: © VCX. Page 103: © VCA. Page 104: © VCA.
Page 106: © VCA. Page 107: Courtesy of Richard Pacheco. Pages 108–109: © VCA. Page 110:
Photo by Julian Wasser/Time Life Pictures/Getty Images. Page 111: © VCA. Page 112: © VCA.
Page 113: © Mike Simons/CORBIS. Page 114: © Rufus F. Folkks/CORBIS. Page 115: © VCA.
Pages 116–117: © Digital Playground. Pages 118–119: © Digital Playground. Pages 120–121: ©
Digital Playground. Page 122: Everett Collection. Page 125: Photo by Author (Avalon); ©
Digital Playground (Andrews). Page 128: © Digital Playground. Page 129: © Private. Page 130:
© Homegrown Video. Page 131: © Adam and Eve. Page 132: © Private. Page 134: © Filmco.
Page 135: © Adam & Eve. Page 136: © Filmco. Page 137: © Private. Page 138: © Homegrown
Video. Page 140: © Private (Background); © Homegrown Video (Inset). Page 141: Photo by
Author. Page 142: © Ramco Productions. Page 145: Bryn Ashburn. Pages 146–147: ©
Bettman/CORBIS (background); © Viviane Moos/Corbis (inset). Page 149: © VR Innovations.
Page 155: © Reuters/CORBIS (both pictures). Page 157: © CORBIS SYGMA. Page 158:
Author. Page 161: © Tokyo Damage Report. Page 162: © Todd Haimann/CORBIS. Page 164: ©
Homegrown Video. Page 165: © Darren Staples/Reuters/Corbis. Page 190: © Digital
Playground. Page 191: © VCA. Page 192: © Private (Leash). Page 193: Photo by Author
(Huffing). Front cover photos: (top left, top middle, and bottom right) © Digital Playground;
(top right) © VCX; (bottom left) © VCA. Spine photo: © Private. Back cover photos: (left)
Library of Congress; (middle) © Digital Playground; (right) The X-Rated Collection.

☆ acknowledgments

This book wouldn't have been possible without the support of my incredibly loving, incredibly tolerant wife, Erin—whose living room was filled with stacks of dirty movies and "boom-chicka-chicka" music for more than a year. (Thanks for pretending not to mind, honey.) They say you never forget your first editor, so I'm grateful mine was Jason Rekulak, who offered guidance, encouragement, and who never flinched—even when I sent images that would've made a lesser man's soul evaporate. And speaking of images, Bryn Ashburn took eleven or twelve pages of text and turned them into this glistening marvel of design in your unworthy hands. Joe Borgenicht brought me into the Quirkiverse, where David Borgenicht decided (I'm still not sure why) to let me write a book. I thank all of them.

I also want to thank the men and women of adult film, who generously donated their time, energy, and knowledge. Especially the endlessly helpful James Avalon, the endlessly kind Kay Taylor Parker and Richard Pacheco, and the endlessly patient Bonnie LeBlanc at VCA. Also taking a bow: Carly Milne and Adella O'Neal, the best publicists in any business. More thanks to Tony Lovett, David at VCX, Dick at Caballero, Ray at Arrow, Steve at Video-X-Pix, Farrell at Homegrown Video, Robert at MBM Media, Chris at Ramco, Jeff at Evil Angel, Scott at Filmco, Joy and Daniel at Wicked, Joone at Digital Playground, Katy at Adam & Eve, and all the fine people at Private.

Also ready for their extreme close-ups: Mindy Brown, Brett Cohen, Erin Slonaker, Emily Betsch, Jessica Pressler, Cele Deemer, and everyone else at Quirk (except you, Mr. Pringles). David "my man in London" Thompson, Steven "my man in Japan" Schultz, and Randy Barbato—for his valuable time and advice. Plus a special thank you to Danielle "The D" Stewart. Finally, I'd like to thank my friends and family—all of whom took my decision to get into porn with grace and dignity.